Links

Ken's Links

Book's Facebook page: https://www.facebook.com/tropnetworking
Tropnetworking, LLC, publishing company, blog and website:
        http://tropnetworking.com/
Ken's Home page: http://kenwalsh.com/

Run With Office, Mahesh and Ken's other book on using Microsoft Office, Web
page: http://runwithoffice.com/
Run With Office Facebook page: https://www.facebook.com/RunWithOffice

Kim and Eric's Links

Dockside Tropical Café Links:
    Web: http://www.docksidetropicalcafe.com/
    Facebook: https://www.facebook.com/DocksideTrop
    Twitter: https://twitter.com/DocksideTrop
    Email: info@docksidetropicalcafe.com
    Yelp: http://www.yelp.com/biz/dockside-tropical-cafe-marathon
    Foursquare: http://4sq.com/18EO7XF *(or use search)*
    Tripadvisor: *use search*

Eric's Other Links:
        Eric's music: http://www.islanderic.com/

Kim's Other Links:
        Kim's yoga web page and blog: http://www.tropicyoga.com/

Dockside

Dockside

Kim and Eric
Embrace Crowdfunding
to Realize Dreams

by Creating
Dockside Tropical Café
Marathon, FL

Kenneth R. Walsh

TropNetworking, LLC
Baton Rouge

Walsh, Kenneth
Dockside: Kim and Eric embrace crowdfunding to realize dreams / Kenneth Walsh.
ISBN-13 978-0-9965535-0-6 (hardback)
ISBN-10 0-996-55350-9 (hardback)

www.tropnetworking.com

Technical Editor, Sathiadev Mahesh
Jacket design by Kenneth R. Walsh

Printed in the United States of America
First American Edition

Contents

List of Figures

List of Tables

Introduction: Crowdfunding as Adventure

The water was clear to the bottom and looked that magical blue you can only see in the islands. Squinting a little in the sun and holding the forestay for balance, I watched the anchor rode glide into its locker. Dan adjusted the dingy line to cruising length. What a great day to be on the water. The motor lightly thumped as we pulled out of Great Harbor in the British Virgin Islands. It seemed a little strange that there was only one other boat still on its mooring ball.

As we cleared Jost Van Dyke, heading for Cane Garden Bay, the rollers came in. It is hard to predict how much a North by North-East wind can kick up the waves between those islands, but the reach of the open water in that direction tends to give them a lift. Standing on the foredeck, I saw what looked to be a wall of water rise before me, so I quickly scooted back to the cockpit. The Beneteau rose smoothly with the wave, but my stomach didn't seem to follow. I glanced at the helm and saw Eric hold his stomach. The boat glided up to the wave's crest and was interrupted by the hard stop of the hull in the next trough which made the standing rigging shake. All of a sudden, the solid 46 footer felt like a homemade dingy against the sea. We watched, in the distance, another cruiser with full sail leaning what looked to be ninety degrees to starboard. The mast didn't touch the water, but I did wonder

1

how the sailors stayed aboard. Maybe we should have stayed put in harbor that day, but we did not, and we were off.

Eric Stone, guitarist, singer, and songwriter, was our captain that week, and his then girlfriend, Kim Hess, was first mate. Eric and Kim had shown us around just the day before. We enjoyed the effervesce of the bubbly pool, which is this cool space between the rocks that fills with seawater at each wave. When the waves smash through the space in the rocks, they leave air bubbles rising up through the pool until the next wave comes along to recharge the process. We even dared sit on the leading rocks and let a few waves wash across us until we visualized what would happen if a slightly larger wave knocked us loose and dragged our bodies across the barnacle covered rocks. Then we jumped back into the middle of the pool, which was safer, and enjoyed those effervesces that made it feel like a natural Jacuzzi. Once we had our fill of bubbles, we walked to Foxy's Taboo for a well-deserved drink after the little hike back. After regaining our energy, we grabbed a cab to the Soggy Dollar bar for a taste of their famous Pain Killer. The Pain Killer, when done right, is topped with fresh ground nutmeg and sipped standing knee deep in the clear waters of White Bay. White Bay seemed like the day spot, but after sunset, people wandered back over a ridge to Great Harbor and stopped at Corsairs, which stayed hopping into the evening. At Corsairs, we met up with the owner, Vinnie, and tossed back some Fireball shots. Those stops at Foxy's, Soggy Dollar, and Corsairs accounted for our late start on that sail, which was why the harbor had been emptied when we awoke. Apparently, the other sailors had not had as much fun as we'd had the night before.

We beat to windward for a couple of hours, mostly staring at the horizon and clenching the rail with white knuckles from time to time. Slowly, the seas eased as we slipped into the shadow of Tortola. The wind and water were calm and seemed to once again be on our side. We pulled into Cane Garden Bay, and the good news was a lot of friends were already there. The bad news was we did not immediately see an empty mooring ball; however, sliding past a few boats and nearing the beach, we finally found a free ball. Eric guided the boat towards the ball while I took the hook to fish the mooring line out of the water. The hook grabbed the line, but didn't slide to the end easily. As the Beneteau drifted past the mooring, my arms were stretched holding on to the hook. By then, we were pulling too hard to shake the hook off the line. With my belly sliced by the toe rail, Kim and Dan holding my ankles, and my forehead just above the water, I was in pain in a lot of strange places. The hook left my hands and floated away, and the Beneteau floated toward the beach. Kim yelled and signaled for Eric to back up. Ed, who was watching the silliness, dingied over and returned our hook. Ed and Kathy had been visiting many of the same ports as us, and we had grown accustomed to seeing the gleaming turquois hull SV Windstar. Ed had restored her with magnificent attention to detail and now hosted guests who were on vacation from the mainland. Knowing his attention to detail only made me more embarrassed about dropping the hook. However, we persevered and executed the maneuver again, with a little better coordination, got a line through the eye, tied it off, and went to the cabin for a decision drink. Decision drinks were a time to sit back, relax, and decide what to do next.

Kim was the beautiful first mate that kept the three of us guys in line. She showed us the knots and checked our work and, at the end of the day, usually came up on deck with a tray full of homemade painkillers that would be the envy of the Soggy Dollar. Kim was an experienced captain herself and, having taken many trips leading boy scouts, was accustomed to guys not listening. Earlier in the trip, I had been thankful when I found out I was assigned to her boat.

Dan Himes, the fourth member of our crew, was from Marblehead, Massachusetts. Having experience with the Power Squadron, he came with a wealth of information.

Captain Woody's voice came across the VHF. "Woody boat to Eric boat, come in."

Eric replied, "This is the Eric Boat."

Sarcastically, Woody continued. "I'm so glad you guys made it. We were worried about you. Have any trouble getting out of Great Harbor?"

"No, we were fine. I thought this was the day we were sleeping in?"

"We all slept in and were on the water by 8 am, but we couldn't seem to raise you on the radio. Anyway, glad you are here now. Are you playing Myett's tonight?"

Eric, his voice re-enthused, said, "You bet we are! Myett's at 6 pm, happy hour, and apps!"

The other boats chimed in as well. "Myett's at 6." A variety of voices was heard, from scratchy old men to giggling girls.

Here you could see the essence of a community: a group of people with a shared love of sailing, naturally drawn to some of the same ports, and glad to help each other. They used VHF radio as their social networking technology to coordinate the adventure.

On January 1, 2012, Kim Hess changed her Facebook relationship status to, "In a relationship with Eric Stone." Eric Stone and Kim Hess were married on April 17, 2013. Two young island visionaries merged their dreams and their fate. Both had been successful in their socially charged careers. Having quit his "day job" back in 1999 when he moved to Nashville, Eric had been touring the US, the islands, and the world for more than fourteen years. Through those years, when the Internet was picking up steam, Eric built mailing lists to keep his fans updated on tour schedules. Kim, an expert in yoga instruction and creator and author of the book and DVD, *Yoga Onboard,* similarly kept her fans updated on her web page. Now they would embark, together, on an adventure that would take them to new heights of love, romance, and social business.

I was fascinated by their journey and wanted to share their amazing accomplishments, energy, and creative ideas with others who may be thinking about taking a similar leap. I cut the dock lines on the book in the summer of 2013 because I needed a little adventure myself and an excuse to get to Marathon more often. In sharing Eric and Kim's story, I wanted to give others a foundation for using some of the same social networking technologies to support their own dreams. Therefore, the book developed a schizophrenic disorder, having both the personality of a rockumentary and a techno-geek how-to book. I didn't know if the multiple personality perspective would work or not, but now that it is done, I can see we have a book rich in detail about both what Kim and Eric went through to make their crowdfund a success and the detail of how to use the technology itself.

This book is full of the technical basics about how webpages, blogs, Facebook, Twitter, email lists, and other related Internet technologies are configured to support business. There are also links to where readers can learn tips on how to search for new information. In future semesters, I will continue teaching about business web technologies at University of New Orleans, so I'll keep blogging about new developments at tropnetworking.com. I hope that this can be a jumping off point for your adventure just as Marathon is for those heading to the Caribbean.

What this book does that no other book does to the same extent is treat social networking technology as a set of integrated tools that work in concert with a community. It also recognizes that you, the potential crowdfunder, are part of a community and your project can gain life through your relationship with your community more than it can through your relationship with your computer tools.

In this book, you will:

- Experience vicariously how Eric and Kim embarked on a rock and roll adventure
- Debunk the myth that social networking is computers, not people
- Understand what crowdfunding technology does and does not do for you
- Understand how your social media plan evolves
- Experience some of the fun along the way
- Envision your own path to social networking technology success

- Get an introduction to the technical details of crowdfunding, social networking, and other Internet technologies so you can begin to do it yourself

A Note about Our Approach to Changes in Prices and Features

For a book about crowdfunding and social networking technologies, changes seem to happen as fast as I can write about them. Many technology books handle this by leaving out specific details and claiming they will keep their blog or web page up-to-date with details after the book is written. This approach presented me with two problems.

First, the devil is in the details. If you omit details, such as today's prices or the features available when the book was written, it can be hard to appreciate why a decision or a recommendation was made. We have decided to quote a number of specific prices, stats, and feature lists that may change by the time you read this. The idea is that you can see the decision process we went through with the information available at the time. If the specifics change, the reader can still use the same process to make decisions appropriate to their circumstances.

Further, it is hard to predict how the technologies will change, which will be important to cover in our blog. Some of the technologies in this book will likely fade from use while others may add so many features that they morph into something new. Those changes will be covered in our blog, but the blog may not be organized in the same way as the book. It will, instead, evolve with the technology.

To use this information in your own situation, you may want to check our blog for updates and check with providers on their latest offerings. Our book will give you the research and decisions processes you can use to come to your own conclusion based on what is currently available. Our web site, TropNetworking.com, will continue to host blogs on exciting new developments, including new or changed crowdfunding platforms, new social networking technologies, or major changes in the currently popular social networking technologies.

Chapter 1: Eric and Kim Craft a Magical Music and Food Venue

The music was hot, the beer was cold, and, yes, it was another day in paradise. I drove straight (ok - a nap on the way) from New Orleans to Salty's in Marathon, Florida, midway out the Keys, to see Eric Stone Band and get some much needed salty water and sunny beaches. I was early and sat down at a table with Eric and Kim. They introduced me to Liz and Rigo, and we all had a coldie. As we sat, chatting and reminiscing about sailing adventures, the crew wandered in. By the time Eric and the band started to play, our table expanded to about eight, and soon after, grew to twelve. After each song, it seemed like another couple came in to join us, leaving us with quite a group.

It was also a treat that night because Eric Stone Band was playing in trio formation. Steve was hammering away on his guitar and Shelley was keeping the beat on congas which were augmented with her occasional high kick to the cymbal. (How does she do that?) Meanwhile, Eric was belting out his own unique form of trop rock.

The fun took a decided uptick in intensity when Eric laid into, "Rock the Dock." Jennifer asked me to dance. Kim rolled tape. I know, I know. There is no tape, but you can't roll a USB drive. Eric sang:

Here's to you. Here's to me.
It's sunny and eighty five.
Here's to us, the lucky ones.
It's sure good to be alive.
We're all here because we're not all there
on Boot Key Harbor today.
Somewhere It's five o'clock, so let's rock the dock
at Dockside Tropical Cafe[1].

The crowd sang, danced, and cheered to that last song of the evening. With the crowdfund still a month away and opening day six months away, the Dockside Tropical Café fantasy was alive in the hearts of fans.

After the gig, we headed back to the boat, and Eric lamented that he still need $100,000 to really pull this off, exclaiming, "Do you have any idea what a tiki roof costs? Tomorrow, we have to edit this film for the Fundable presentation." I pointed out that tomorrow, he would be playing the marina bar while I was boiling the crawfish, but on the day after that, we could get back to video.

Mentally reviewing his to-do list, eyes glazed over, Eric continued. "And oh man, we have to get all this together before we leave on the summer tour at the end of the month."

The Fundable video presentation would be one of the ways Eric and Kim would communicate their story before, during, and after the Fundable campaign. Fundable is one of several new breeds of fundraising websites that seeks to capitalize on the reach of the Web to bring large groups of small investors and donors to support projects. Projects come in a wide variety of types, ranging from charitable efforts to business start-ups and expansions. Types of support can range from donations to prepaid merchandise, and even equity investments. What the sites have in common is that a significant project is proposed to the community, fundraising targets are set, and by using the tools of the web, a geographically dispersed audience can participate and track the project's progress. The concept of raising money by means of many small funders is not new, but the level of accessibility to the tool by the small artist or entrepreneur is greatly enhanced with Internet-based technologies. The time it takes to raise, collect, and put to work funds is greatly reduced through using a net-based crowdfunding platform. However, as you read more about how Eric and Kim worked with their community to develop their campaign, you will realize a lot more time is needed, both before and after the time of the campaign itself. Although the campaign may be a mere thirty days, the preparation needed to be successful might take months or even a lifetime when you consider, as we will in the following chapters, how Eric has developed his music career and relationship with his fans. After the campaign ends, the real "fun" can begin. This includes completing the project, fulfilling the rewards, and tacking onto a new course. Crowdfunders need to have all their ducks in a row even before they start the funding process, and they need to be prepared to put on their project manager hats immediately after the funds come in. Being a project manager entails dealing with multiple suppliers and service providers in order to stay on track and completing the project successfully, within budget, and on time. This means crowdfunders need to put together a complete project plan before they start the crowdfunding process. In addition, there is one other challenge in crowdfunding. Most crowdfunding projects raise funds by offering pre-paid coupons for services or keepsakes. These patrons must be provided with the tangible products or services they were promised. The fulfillment process is time consuming, and tracking the delivery of rewards can be a full-time job that requires advance planning.

The following are examples of the range of projects that can be funded with crowdfunding: Susan Lee raised $581 to produce her play, "Diary of a Mid-Life Crisis" (Knowledge@Wharton, 2010), while Spike Lee recently raised $M1.4 for his new film project, "The Newest Hottest Spike Lee Joint" (Lee, 2013). I don't know if $581 would be enough to help with my mid-life crisis, but it couldn't hurt.

Preparing for Fundable Crowdfunding

The first fundraising step Eric and Kim would take would be through a crowdfunding company called Fundable. I asked Eric why he chose Fundable, and he said their ability to design the plan for the entire campaign looked like it would result in better success than a site that just provided the technology.

With Fundable, and often with other crowdfunding sites, a campaign is established which defines a timeframe, a goal, and incentives. The set timeframe is a necessary requirement for effective crowdfunding. There are basically two groups of investors who participate in crowdfunding. The first group includes individuals who are part of the core community and have confidence in the entrepreneur's ability to succeed in the venture. Their investment is a vote of confidence in the project. The second group includes investors on the fringes of the community – think friends of friends in a social network as well as complete outsiders who are drawn in by the project's initial success. The second tier of investors will participate only if the first group raises a sufficient level of investment to create an aura of success for the project. The short time frame, typically thirty days, creates sufficient viral buzz around the project in the secondary group to achieve the target. Fundable advised Eric that a modest goal could help create buzz, allow him to capture some funding (even if not enough), and would have the potential to "blow by the initial goal." Eric set his initial goal at $25,000, knowing that it would be possible to move forward with that amount although it would also result in possibly foregoing some of the improvements to Dockside until they could be funded by cash flow. Of course, reaching $50,000 to $75,000 would make for a more solid start.

The Fundable site for Dockside Tropical Café is hosted by Fundable, and Fundable has an architecture for crowdfunding which includes features for collecting pledge information, monitoring progress, and collecting funds through successful campaigns. However, a client organization, such as Dockside Tropical Café, still needs to develop a complete storyboard for the campaign. This includes a well-developed story of why the fundraising is needed and what will be accomplished with the funds. Some of this may require soul searching. What is your vision, and who will be helped if you achieve your vision? You might also ask, how does this vision fit within the community? Many crowdfunding proposals use short stories with brief presentations designed to capture and hold investor interest. Due to the large number of crowdfunding projects, short blurbs were seen as more effective than long proposals. When the dot-com boom took place at the turn of the millennium, the rush of new ideas resulted in the one-minute elevator pitch – a short, highly focused pitch that could grasp a venture capitalist's interest. With the new funding model all set to replace the old guard, arguments were raised that the traditional business plan was dead. The dot-com bust that quickly followed cleared up the air and business funding, reverting to the thorough, well laid out business plan. As the crowdfunding model evolves, it is highly likely that more organized, well designed proposals that communicate not only the vision, but also the ability of the promoter to successfully complete the project, along with testimonials from respected trust agents, will become an integral part of a crowdfunding proposal. While the crowdfunding platform may limit the length of on-platform proposals, external links to sites with more information about the project and its promoters should be a part of the story. Note that much of the crowdfunding investment will come from members of the online community closely linked to the project.

Eric and Kim developed a site that told their story in words, pictures, and video. A video was shot that brought their vision to life for the viewer. Location was important to them, so highlights of their location in Marathon, Florida, took center stage. The video also included a personal appeal where Eric and Kim explained how the vision was developed and how they would bring it to life. The appeal showed how fans could become part of the vision by pledging for the incentives.

Many prominent supporters and fans of the project were included in the video and in photographs on the site. Eric's bandmates, Steve and Shelley, talked from a musician's point of view about how great it would be to have a high quality music venue in Marathon. To have another place that could serve as a potential gig on the way to Key West, located in a waterside venue with a premium sound system, would be a treasure for trop rock musicians.

In addition to compelling content, the menu of incentives needs to be carefully developed. Eric and Kim developed a menu of incentives that considered their fans' interests and values and that offered a range of price points. The incentives included products that Eric and Kim knew they could deliver at the times promised. One good example of matching cost effectiveness with high value is the download of Eric's complete CD collection. At little marginal cost to produce, it provides good value to Eric's fans, who would love to have the complete collection in one place. It probably does not result in lost sales, since those same fans have probably purchased some of his music products in the past. Further, the fans have now become even greater word of mouth advocates for the music, and that's really how the band made it this far anyway. Likewise, the bar tabs become a fair and fun way to get started. Significant operating capital for supplies and expenses will be needed until it is covered by cash flow, and the bar tabs prepay the patrons' purchase to match that need. An important issue regarding the pre-paid tabs is the need to treat this as a liability of the business. Serious consideration must be given to the expiration date for any coupons, and an adequate security mechanism must be selected to ensure the validity of the coupons. However, patrons must know that by paying in advance, Dockside will be fully stocked and ready to roll when they arrive. The extra incentives are great, too.

T-shirts and hats were yet other incentives. Eric designed the new logo for Dockside to be used on signs, advertising, and merchandise, so he incorporated the new logo into the t-shirts and hats. As an extra touch, he labeled them as "Charter Crew," so fans could display their support as an early adopter. See Table 1 for the complete list of incentives developed for the Fundable campaign.

Table 1: List of Incentive used for Fundable Campaign

Funding Level	Incentive
$15	A personal thank you postcard from the beautiful Florida Keys signed by Eric and Kim Stone PLUS digital download of Eric's unreleased Dockside theme song: "Rock The Dock"
$50	The $15 level PLUS Dockside Tropical Café charter crew t-shirt
$100	The $50 level PLUS Eric Stone's complete cd collection (digital download) PLUS Recognition on "wall of fame"
$250	The $100 level PLUS "Crew Card" – 5% off up to 4 people for life* PLUS $200 bar tab*
$500	The $100 level PLUS "Crew Card" – 10% off up to 4 people for life* PLUS $400 bar tab*
$1000	The $100 level PLUS "Crew Card" – 15% off up to 4 people for life* PLUS $800 bar tab*
$2500	The $100 level PLUS "Crew Card" – 20% off up to 4 people for life* PLUS $2000 bar tab* PLUS Personalized Tiki Bar Stool
$5000	The $100 level PLUS "Crew Card" – 20% off up to 4 people for life* PLUS $4000 bar tab* PLUS Personalized restaurant table
$10000	The $100 level PLUS "Crew Card" – 20% off up to 4 people for life* PLUS $8000 bar tab* PLUS We will name a specialty drink after you PLUS Personalized "front row seating" (business or personal) (front row seating = 2 seats/cocktail table around dance floor)
	*Crew Cards and bar tabs to be used with no other offers and limited to $200 per day.

The Crowdfunding Myth

The conventional wisdom in crowdfunding sometimes describes the process as one where the prospective fundraiser designs and implements its crowdfunding site then communicates the site widely and receives funding. A conventional approach might look like that shown in Figure 1. Although there is some logic to this approach, it misses the richness of the community in which your crowdfunding effort is embedded and treats it as a finite activity. The steps outlined on both the Fundable site, which Eric used, and Kickstarter, another popular crowdfunding site, both have this simplification. In this model, what is left out is the fundraiser's ability to bring the community in as partners on the project, participating and having their ideas not only heard, but also informing the crowfund plans.

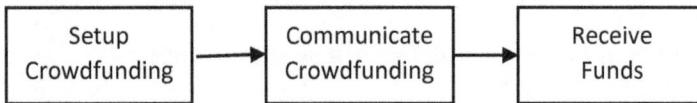

```
┌──────────────┐      ┌──────────────┐      ┌──────────────┐
│    Setup     │      │ Communicate  │      │   Receive    │
│ Crowdfunding │─────▶│ Crowdfunding │─────▶│    Funds     │
└──────────────┘      └──────────────┘      └──────────────┘
```

Figure 1: Conventional Crowdfunding Process

In an interview with Forbes, Slava Rubin, one of the founders of Indiegogo, described the relationship between the project and the crowdfund this way:

> The worst thing is for people to think that just if you build it, they will come. Indiegogo by itself does not automatically create a great business. What entrepreneurs need to do, or anybody who's pushing forward or campaigning on Indiegogo, is they need to get that ball rolling and they need to be serious about their effort. Indiegogo helps amplify all that to get the word out and help them raise more money than they ever could on their own.[2]

A better approach is to realize that the crowdfunding effort is embedded in your community and needs understanding of that community's interests and roles. The community can then become partners with the project. For descriptive purposes, we can describe a pre-crowdfunding phase consisting of the following steps: foster community, discuss crowdfunding, and setup crowdfunding.

Early crowdfunding success stories, like the stars of the early dot-com boom, worked with a range of approaches. However, as the model matures and the number of crowdfunding projects rises, new project promoters need to foster the community. Of course, when Spike Lee raised 1.4 million dollars for his rather vaguely worded crowdfunded movie project, his success was almost entirely due to his pre-existing off-line reputation. The crowdfunding platform merely offered a convenient, web-based means to organize the flow of money. A project promoter with a more limited off-line presence needs to get involved in an online community and become an effective participant. The promoter can leverage off-line reputation to build online community reputation. Online communities, like real world communities, need a raison-d'etre. They can be based on a shared interest, such as music genre or technology interest, they can provide gaming entertainment, offer a platform to support trade, or they can extend an off-line community separated by geography. The project promoter need not initially create and build the community; rather, it is important that he or she participates and contributes to the community. This step will become even more important in the process as crowdfunding becomes more pervasive and being heard above the chatter becomes more difficult.

Next, we can describe the crowdfunding event itself and a post-crowdfunding phase called Developing the Project. Each of these phases describes a continuous and rich interaction with the community. Again, for descriptive purposes, this model is shown in Figure 2; however, one should note that some of the activities are ongoing and parallel rather than sequential.

```
┌─────────────────┐
│     Foster      │ ┐
│    Community    │ │
└─────────────────┘ │
        │           │
        ▼           │
┌─────────────────┐ │
│     Discuss     │ ├──  Pre-Crowdfunding Phase
│   Crowdfunding  │ │
└─────────────────┘ │
        │           │
        ▼           │
┌─────────────────┐ │
│      Setup      │ │
│   Crowdfunding  │ ┘
└─────────────────┘

        │
        ▼
┌─────────────────┐ ┐
│   Communicate   │ ├──  Crowdfunding Active Phase
│   Crowdfunding  │ ┘
└─────────────────┘

        │
        ▼
┌─────────────────┐ ┐
│  Receive Funds  │ │
│   and Fulfill   │ │
│     Rewards     │ │
└─────────────────┘ ├──  Post-Crowdfunding Phase
        │           │
        ▼           │
┌─────────────────┐ │
│     Extend      │ │
│  Community and  │ │
│ Continue Project│ ┘
└─────────────────┘
```

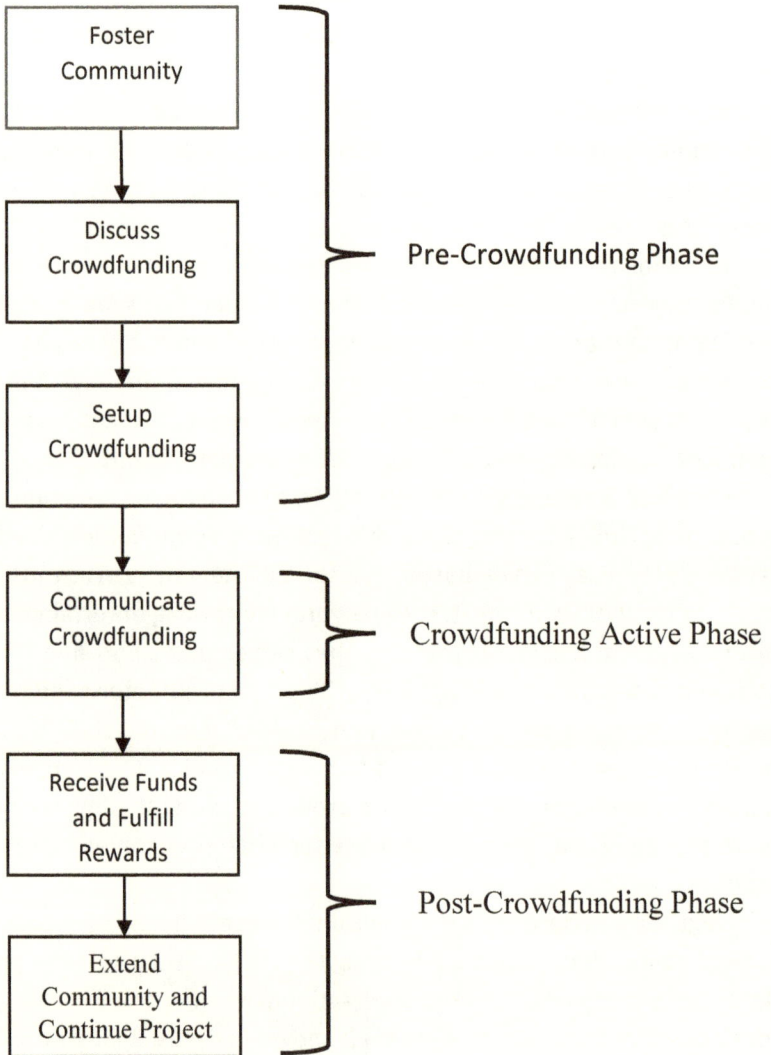

Figure 2: An Inclusive Crowdfunding Approach

Pre-Crowdfunding Phase

In the Pre-Crowdfunding Phase, one looks at where the community might stand in terms of understanding the project, how to discuss the project with them, and ways to develop the crowdfunding concept. The possibility of crowdfunding for a project must be presented to the community to solicit members' opinions and suggestions. The idea is to find out if the community believes that this is a suitable project for crowdfunding.

Does the community have the ability to raise significant funds for the project, which will assist in the secondary fundraising process, and does the community believe the project promoter's ability to deliver on the project? To what extent does the community understand the current project? This project may be a logical extension of what you or your organization has been doing or it may be somewhat of a departure. However, in either case, the need for crowdfunding must at least be a new phase in your work. So first, discuss with your community the new project and ask for their feedback on how the project is unfolding. See to what extent their ideas can be included. What areas would you need their input, and what areas would you rather rely on your own professional judgment?

Areas where you need to exercise professional judgment may be good areas to develop a blog where you can produce useful information for your community while also showing them how you will apply that knowledge to you project. In this case, you are providing benefits to your community before asking them for anything.

In areas where there can be some alternatives to the project that your community can help shape, foster discussions so you can hear what the community prefers. Eric's Facebook posting of potential menu items for Dockside would make your mouth water. Eric and Kim both like to cook, and in the months leading up to the crowdfund and continuing through opening the restaurant, they posted many of their lushest inventions. (Hey, gotta eat!) Integrating what you already do in your life, while still communicating with your community, can make your project more fun. It shouldn't feel like a chore. And this is important since your readers/viewers will soon realize whether you actually enjoy what you do or if you are just another paid grunt, churning out words for a fee.

In addition to discussing the project, it is critical to discuss what crowdfunding is and how it fits in with the overall project. Many in the community may not know much about crowdfunding at all, and if they do, there are so many variations that fall under the broad umbrella of crowdfunding that they may not understand how it applies to your project. Finally, and this is certain to become more of an issue as crowdfunding expands, there is the fact that potential investors may have experienced a failure with a crowdfunding project before. A potential investor who has been burned in a crowdfunding failure before, albeit one that may have been a complete scam or more likely a complete mismanagement, will flee from an online community that solicits crowdfunding. Over time and as the market evolves, it will be necessary to describe the project in greater detail to potential funders and to lay out a complete project plan that demonstrates competence in completing the project successfully.

The FAQ's on some crowdfunding sites and books seem to suggest that funders should develop their crowdfund site and then use social networking to drive traffic to the site. Although that is part of the story, the community involvement in the project, as well as planning the crowdfund long before it is initiated, may be more important.

On August 22, 2013, I texted Eric on this section of the book and on the importance of the community involvement, pre-crowdfund.

He texted back, "**True**," and I promised to bold it. He followed up, expanding:

> We started telling people we were gonna do a crowdfund months before we went live. Much of my discussions were educating what and how crowdfund works. One of those people who'd never heard of crowdfunding became a $2500.00 pledger.

The funder needs to describe for the community how the fund will enhance the project, including details of what will be accomplished by the funding. It may be useful to describe what can be accomplished at different levels of funding. Note that this should also be approached as

18

a discussion because the community will have ideas on how to shape the project. In effect, what is necessary is that you do not become the sole promoter of the project. Rather, you are the initiator of the project, but the community supports your goal for the project and carries it forward. From a fundraising perspective, one of the reasons that many successful projects have dealt with the arts is that the community gains from the completion of the art project. Helping you convert your attic into a man-cave does not translate into community well-being, unless, of course, the community is made up of future regulars to the facility.

Finally, discuss the rewards structure you propose. You do not want, on the opening day of the fundraising campaign, for your community to see the reward structure for the first time. They may not have been thinking in the same terms you were. You are living the project and know what you want, but you do not want the community to be blindsided by what you ask. Prior to the Crowdfunding Active Phase, vet the reward structure and solicit ideas for revision and added levels. If you know your community well, you may realize that different rewards appeal to different segments of the community.

Crowdfunding Active Phase

During the active phase, it is, of course, important to communicate with the community the status of the fundraising in terms of reaching the goal, but also what will happen as milestones are reached or new developments in the project are developed.

Eric kept his fans up-to-date throughout the crowdfund. On July 15, Eric released a new podcast that described the state of the Fundable campaign and introduced the idea of how an equity campaign would follow. Since the podcast is audio, in a radio like format, Eric could also include the song "Rock the Dock," making for a complete picture of the business and entertainment sides of the venture.

The Summer 2013 Tour

The Fundable site went live on June 19, 2013, just as Eric, Kim, and Steve began their summer tour with a recording session in Nashville. They would need to be in Nashville, Tennessee, by June 20 for a recording session and then off to Rockville, Indiana, by June 22 for the first show of the summer tour. The tour included seven states – Indiana, Illinois, Wisconsin, California, Idaho, Montana, and Washington – and twenty-three shows over the next seven weeks. The Fundable campaign would begin and either succeed or fail all while being managed during the road trip. The Summer 2013 Tour Schedule is shown in Table 2. If you think it would be difficult to keep up the communication during your crowdfund, take inspiration from this schedule.

Table 2: Summer Tour Schedule, 2013

Date	Start Time	City, State	Event
6/20		Nashville, TN	Kenny Royster's Direct Image Recording Studio
6/22	6:00 pm	Rockville, IN	Racoon Lake, Racoon Lake Party
6/23	1:00 pm	Bismarck, IL	Seilder's Pool Party
6/29	7:00 pm		Jeremy & Nam's House Party
7/1	5:00 pm	Bayfield, WI	Bayfield Sail Week
7/2	8:00 pm	Bayfield, WI	Bayfield Sail Week, Bayfield Inn
7/3	6:00 pm	Bayfield, WI	Bayfield Sail Week, Tiki Bar Superior Yacht Charters
7/4	7:00 pm	Bayfield, WI	Bayfield Sail Week, Bayfield Inn
7/5	6:00 pm	New Germany, MN	Down South Bar & Grill
7/6	6:00 pm	Long Beach, CA	Navy Yacht Club 4th of July Party
7/12	8:00 pm	Ririe, ID	Old Ririe Bar
7/13	7:00 pm	West Yellowstone, MT	Buffalo Bar & Casino
7/14	4:00 pm	West Yellowstone, MT	Buffalo Bar & Casino
7/17	6:00 pm	West Yellowstone, MT	Buffalo Bar & Casino
7/18	6:00 pm	West Yellowstone, MT	Buffalo Bar & Casino
7/19	6:00 pm	West Yellowstone, MT	Buffalo Bar & Casino
7/26	5:00 pm	McCall, ID	Mile High Marina
7/28		Reno, NV	Jalapeno Rays' House Party
8/2	7:00 pm	McCall, ID	Mill Harbor Yacht Club
8/3	5:00 pm	McCall, ID	Mile High Marina
8/4	4:00 pm	Lewiston, ID	McRobert's House Concert
8/9	5:00 pm	Seattle, WA	PHOPS Tin Cup Chalice
8/10	6:00 pm	Poulsbo, WA	Cruising Outpost PNW Cruisers Bash
8/11	2:00 pm	Seattle, WA	Alicia Smith's House

Kim did a great job of Facebooking the interesting stops on the tour, supporting the music fan base, and keeping up interest in the Fundable campaign. For example, on June 27, her FaceBook page documents a "shark attack" at the Jimmy Buffet concert in Indiana, including a picture of her, Eric, Steve, and friends. A "shark attack" is a gathering of Jimmy Buffett fans, and Kim and Eric were happy to have a brief break from the tour and just hang out as fans. Between June 19 and August 7, Kim made twenty-one original posts to her page, including great pictures of locations on the tour and meetings with friends and family along the way.

Crowdfunding Results

Amazingly, on June 25, six days after launching the Fundable site, Dockside had reached its initial goal of $25,000. Although the figure was originally set on the low side so that the project could carry on, achieving the initial goal so quickly was an encouraging triumph. After the $25,000 was reached, Eric described a stretch goal of $50,000 and described to fans how that would benefit the project. Fans responded well. The stretch goal was achieved, followed by a new stretch target of $75,000. Table 3 shows the total amount raised for each incentive, as well as the overall total, making for an extraordinary thirty days.

Table 3: Amounts at each incentive level as of 8/6/2013

Funding Level	Number	Total
$15	15	$225
$50	23	$1,150
$100	61	$6,100
$250	65	$16,250
$500	17	$8,500
$1000	9	$9,000
$2500	7	$17,500
$5000	1	$5,000
$10000	0	$0
Total	198	$63725

As of 8/6/2013, the Fundable site ended the incentive phase of crowdfunding. Since the original $25,000 was surpassed, Fundable charged the respective donors, collected the money, and submitted it to Eric and Kim, minus fees. Of course, many fans were still eager to be involved with the incentive phase. The same set of incentives could still be purchased using PayPal from either Dockside's or Eric's IslandEric.com music homepage. Again, not commonly addressed in crowdfunding FAQ's, the rewards program does not have to end at the end of the crowdfund timeframe. It may be appropriate to continue after through web pages and paypal or other eCommerce sites.

We analyzed data on the pledges in two ways: by day of campaign and by day of week. Since this study was exploratory, no final conclusion can be reached, but it does give insight into some areas to consider in practice as well as where more controlled research could be conducted.

Figure 3 shows the number of rewards per day in the forty-one day campaign, and Figure 4 shows the total dollar amount pledged per day. Clearly, there was more activity in the beginning and ending days of the campaign. It is likely that the campaign kickoff in the beginning, and the reminders of the campaign's ending at the end, were the best times to hold fans' attention. At this point, we can just describe the pattern. However, we do not have enough information to know to what extent this may be a natural flow versus this being a result of the social networking campaign that was on-going in support of the crowdfund. Note the wide variation in busy days and slow days.

Figure 3: Number of Rewards by Day in Campaign

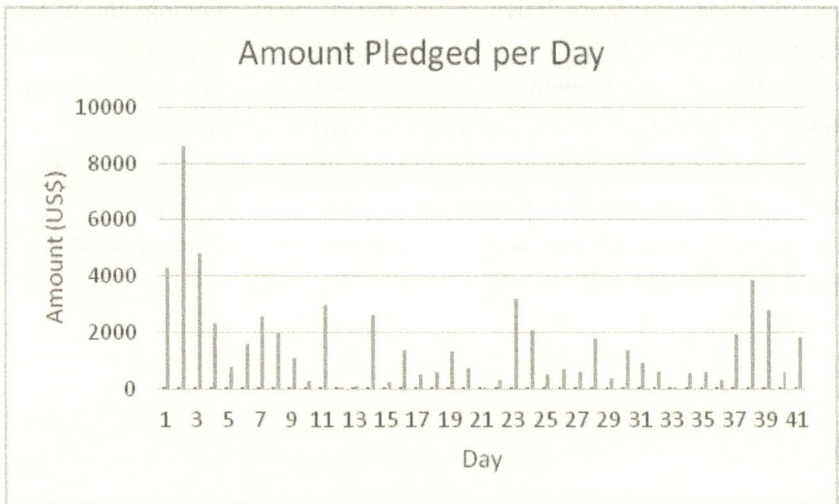

Figure 4: Total Amount Pledged by Day in Campaign

Figure 5 shows the average number of rewards per day of week, and Figure 6 shows the average amount of pledges per day of week. This data makes Thursday appear to be the most active day of the week for crowdfunding. Again, because this was not a controlled study, the cause is unknown. Days do appear to have different patterns, but it would be good to correlate with social networking promotional levels which were not scheduled systematically apriori.

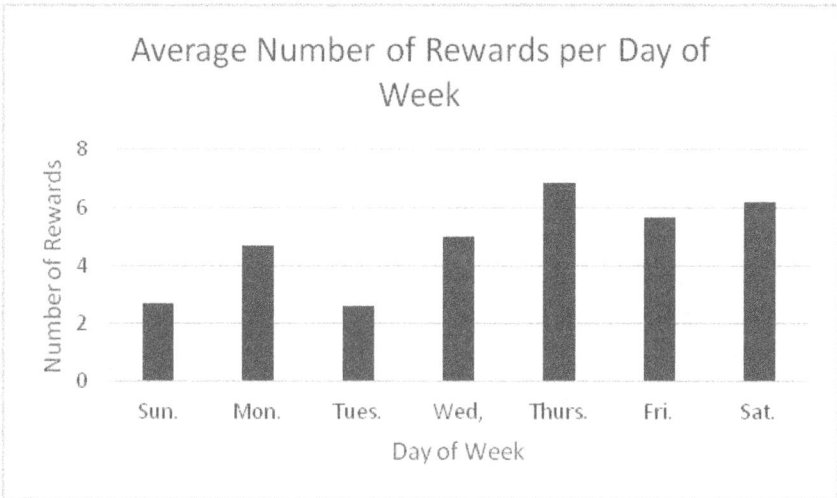

Figure 5: Average Number Rewards Sold by Day Of Week

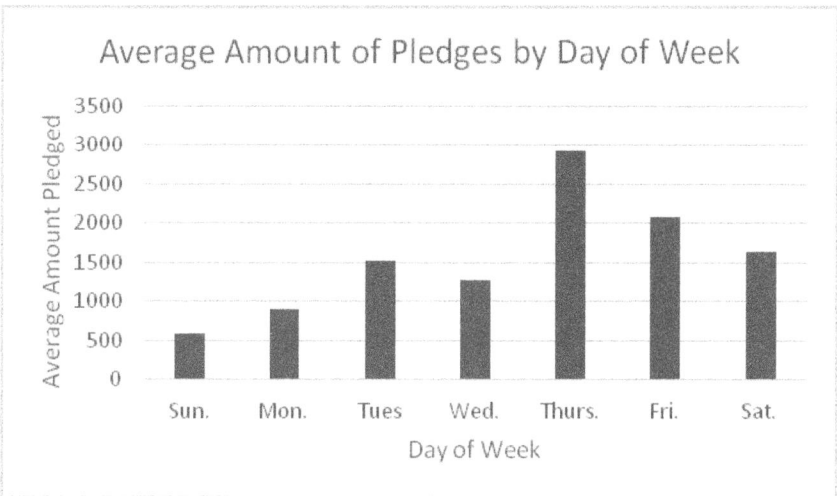

Figure 6: Average Amount a Pledges by Day of Week

Tequila Investing

On August 6, 2013, the Fundable site transitioned from an incentive site to an investor site. Crowdfunding for equity investment is significantly different than for rewards because of the SEC regulations involved. In fact, those regulations are being rewritten as this book is being written.

After launching the investment phase and finishing the summer tour, Kim and Eric headed back for Marathon. On the road home, they scheduled a stop in Dallas with Bob Appel, both fan and potential investor. Eric had met Bob several years earlier in St. Thomas. Bob had flown in to do a little sailing and trop rocking with his high school friend, Brian Watson. Brian was a big fan of Eric's and had introduced Bob to the music.

It turned out that Bob was an investor and may have been interested in Eric and Kim's new adventure. Eric made the pitch, and Bob looked into the opportunity. Bob was impressed with Eric and Kim's commitment and could see Eric's flare for marketing. He was also well aware of the risk of startups in the restaurant and bar businesses. Many failed, and those which did well could still take years for the investment pay off. After a visit to Marathon and some heart to heart talks, Bob decided to offer a line of credit that would get the doors open, provide operating funds to give it a chance, and let Kim and Eric remain full owners. Of course, there was one important condition: the bar had to serve Herradura Seleccion Suprema!

Post-Crowdfunding Phase

Beginning August 20, Eric and Kim were back in Marathon, for the most part. Still playing at the boat shows and some other Keys, they could focus more on the work at hand: finishing Dockside. Balancing many aspects of the business is truly the life of the entrepreneur. Eric would be knee-deep in paint part of the day, then would have to drive to that other Key and belt out some of that other guy's songs. Through the end of August and throughout September, Eric and Kim posted a number of Facebook updates. Some examples are listed in Table 4. The postings included a mix of construction updates and other related activities.

Table 4: *Status Updates on the Dockside Facebook Page*

Date	Description	Category	Likes
8/20	Announced Return to Marathon	Related Event	8
8/23	Dockside Renovation 1	Const. Update	65
8/29	Reminder on how to purchase rewards	Crowdfund	5
9/1	New hurricane shutter (w/ 8/23 post)	Const. Update	n/a
9/3	Reference Underwater Sombrero Book	Related event	10
9/5	Eric painting the window trim in some kool colors and patterns	Const. Update	114
9/7	Glycol and treasure chest	Const. Update	65
9/8	iPad driven mixing board	Const. Update	23
9/18	Visitors from the Caribbean	Related Event	38
9/18	Visitors from the Caribbean Part 2	Related Event	36
9/19	Arial View Of Dockside	Const. Update	17
9/21	American Idol Joke (shows deck, stage, and fun people in pics.)	Const. Update	80
(Post Crowdfund, 8/20/2013-9/21/2013, likes updated 1/6/2014)			

The Crowdfunding Industry

The crowdfunding industry has become an important and fast growing segment of social network technology and is significant in that it provides a direct link between a social networking community and financing efforts. According to the Massolution crowdfunding industry report, "Crowdfunding platforms raised $2.7 billion (an 81% increase) and successfully funded more than 1 million campaigns in 2012. Massolution forecasts an increase in global crowdfunding volumes in 2013, to $5.1 billion."[3] Crowdsourcing.org, the major industry organization for crowdfunding organizations, lists 2,478 crowdfunding sites[4].

Kickstarter stands out as the name often associated with creating the crowdfunding phenomena. "In 2012 alone, more than 2.2 million people backed a Kickstarter project."[5]

Table 5 and Table 6 list twenty interesting crowdfunding sites in alphabetical order. As with many of the technologies explored in this book, we will not list the top ten examples, with number one being best, for a couple of reasons. The main reason is that beauty is in the eye of the beholder, and many of the examples are best for particular situations. To clarify this, we will discuss the various features or criteria of examples that makes them more or less suitable for particular situations. The second reason is that the sites or technologies we might be discussing change frequently in the Internet era. When we describe examples, and which may be best for particular situations, we will try to explain our thought process so you can modify or even disagree with it as it applies to the situation you might be facing. Further, since you will be reading this in the future, after I have written it (unless you are the NSA, who may have tapped my laptop and can read it before its published!), the world will have changed. You will still need to check out what is currently available, and we want to let you know the "why" behind our thinking to see if our reasoning still applies. Later in the book, I will compare web and blog platforms and use a similar philosophy in my presentation.

Although the concept of crowdfunding is applied to both donations and equity investments, the type of projects and the business framework would be completely different in the two categories. We have divided the crowdfunding into three major classes: donations, rewards, and investment.

In the donations class, the person or organization is seeking a donation of funds to support a good cause. The causes, of course, are quite varied, and may include relief for victims of a disaster, help for a needy group, funds for surgery for an individual, or protection of an endangered species. The organizations conducting the fundraising might be an individual or a non-profit organization organized under IRS code

501c3. In this case, the primary motivation is for the donors to help the needs of the recipients or to help a cause proposed by the organization.

In the rewards class, the person or organization seeking funding to develop a new product or work of art is seeking capital to cover development costs. From a CD or book, to a high tech gadget or new web service, the products themselves vary widely. In this case, the donors are supporters of the new product idea and want to be a part of it coming to market. The donors, in this case, are often buying rewards or prepaid products. Rewards may be extra perks that come with the product, such as autographs, custom versions of the product, or even dinner with the developer. Prepaids include paying for the product before it is developed so that the funds can be used for production costs. In this case, the organization is often for-profit and is trying to launch either its first product or a product that is much bigger than ones in the past. The person or organization could be non-profit as well, and, for example, be developing a work of art for a public gallery. The Fundable site states that a rewards campaign will typically be less than $50,000. Campaigns looking for more than $50,000 are more likely to look at the investment type of campaign[6].

In the investment class, the person or organization is seeking funds either for new product development, to start a business, or expand business. In this case, they are willing to share an equity stake in the organization in exchange for the investment. Here, the investor is seeking to help the project succeed but is also likely looking for a return on investment. The organizations seeking this type of funding are likely to be for-profit and are looking at product categories that benefit society but also include potential for profits and growth.

Although all three types of crowdfunding seek patron support, the expectations of the patron and the legal and business structure of the organizations are much different. In the case of donations, it is important to have a non-profit business, and it is important that donated funds reach the intended cause with minimal overhead. The donor, in this case, is less interested in a concrete reward but rather in an efficient use of funds to best support the stated recipient. In the case of rewards program, the donors are helping the project because they think the new product would be valuable to society, but also to them individually. They would expect a rewards structure which lets them be involved in some way with the product, either at the front end, in products ideas, or the back end, in custom version of the product. In the last case, the donor is interested in return on investment as well as the benefit of the product and will most likely be investing a more significant amount of funds that needs to be protected. Equity investments also fall under much stricter regulation in terms of the definitions of the investment, who can invest, and who an investor can solicit.

The second two classes, rewards and investment, can easily work together; however, the separation must be clear to all involved. For example, there could be a rewards program for a product, wherein the rewards donor receives a customer product, in conjunction with an investment program, wherein the donor gains an equity stake. Although the donation type would not have the same overlap, some type of reward to the donor may be involved. The monetary value of the reward would typically be kept small so that most funds would be targeted at the project.

With the vastly different goals of these three classes of crowdfunding, the support needed from the crowdfunding provider varies substantially and makes for a good way to organize the providers in the industry. In particular, equity investing has more substantial tax and SEC implications.

Another way sites may vary is in whether or not it is necessary to reach a funding goal for the funding to be consummated. In many projects, it may make sense to have minimum goal or the project cannot be created. For example, if a new product has certain start-up costs, it may not be feasible to produce in small numbers, as there may not be a way to fulfill the prepaid obligation to a small number of donors. In that type of campaign, the donors would not be charged if the campaign fell short of its goal. For prepaids and investments, this type is also useful for the project owner to decide what minimum start up might make the project worthwhile. Kickstarter, for example, states that 44% of campaigns meet their minimum[7]. When using a required minimum amount, the project owner may want to set the minimum low to increase the chance of achieving it. In this scenario, it may be possible to collect much more money than the minimum, and the project owner would want to develop and communicate stretch goals where he or she articulates what additional products or features could be developed if the campaign reaches higher goal levels. In the case of the donation campaign, often any amount can be helpful to the cause and a project minimum is not needed. Indiegogo, for example, allows the funders to choose whether or not they set a minimum.

Table 5: 20 Interesting Crowdfunding Sites (site name)

Funding Site	Site Name	Year Founded	Types of Projects
AngelList	angel.com	2010	Start-ups
ArtistShare	artistshare.net	2001	Artistic Works
Authr	authr.com	2011	Writing
Causes	causes.com	2007	Fundraising
Crowdfunder	crowdfunder.com	2011	Start-ups
Crowdrise	crowdrise.com	2009	Charitable Cause
CrowdTilt	crowdtilt.com	2012	Small Community Fundraising
EquityNet	equitynet.com	2005[8]	Start-ups
FirstGiving	firstgiving.com		Fundraising
Fundable	fundable.com	2012	Start-ups
Fundly	fundly.com	2009	Fundraising
FundRazr	fundrazr.com	2010	Fundraising
GiveForward	giveforward.com	2008	Medical fundraising
GoFundMe	gofundme.com	2010	Fundraising
IndieGoGo	indiegogo.com	2008	Any
Kickstarter	kickstarter.com	2009	Creative Works
Quirky	quirky.com	2009	New products
Razoo	razoo.com	2006	Charity and personal fundraising
RocketHub	rockethub.com	2010	Creative projects
YouCaring	youcaring.com	2012	Personal Causes

Table 6: 20 Interesting Crowd Funding Sites (fees and ranking)

Funding Site	Fee*	Alexa Rank (2014)	Alexa Rank, 8/23/2012[9]	Type**
AngelList	n/a	7,131	n/a	I
ArtistShare	30%[10]	630,001	n/a	R
Authr	14.95/month	1,528,033	n/a	R
Causes	4/75%	13,315	n/a	D
Crowdfunder	$99-$999/month	44,913	188,628	I
Crowdrise	1-5%	20,572	n/a	D
CrowdTilt	2.5%	32,094	166,285	D
EquityNet	$19/$29/$69/month	140,627	n/a	I
FirstGiving	5%	65,602	n/a	D
Fundable	$99/month	63,385	96,830	R, I
Fundly	2.9-4.9%	28,273	n/a	D
FundRazr	5%	36,963	n/a	D,R,I
GiveForward	5%	21,889	55,883	D
GoFundMe	5%	1,962	9,896	D
IndieGoGo	4%-9%[11]	1,745	1959	R, D
Kickstarter	5%[12]	610	695	R
Quirky	$99	10,043	n/a	R
Razoo	4.9%	47,978	n/a	D
RocketHub	4-8%	49,686	49,490	R
YouCaring	Free	11,931	n/a	D

*In addition to fees listed, many sites also have merchant fees for credit card processing.
**R=Rewards Class; I=Investment Class; D=Donation

Fundable.com

Eric and Kim chose to go with Fundable.

Fundable was launched on May 22, 2012, with five companies seeking funding[13]. Serial entrepreneurs Wil Schroter and Eric Corl began the platform as a rewards platform, but with change in regulations in regard to marketing to investors, they expanded into equity funding[14]. Their strategy was to be a leader in the investment side of crowdfunding since some of the earlier heavy weights in crowdfunding were staying in rewards and donations.

The ability to conduct both incentive-based and investment-based crowdfunding was one of the reasons Eric and Kim chose Fundable. In the summer of 2013, Fundable was a leading site with support for investor fundraising that would comply with regulations pre-dating the JOBS Act by seeking funds only from qualified investors. The Fundable site asked investors to verify their status as accredited investors before any investment information was shared from firms seeking investors. Eric and Kim began the investor portion of their crowdfund and received favorable responses. After discussions with would-be equity investors, they mutually decided that the partners would offer debt instruments instead.

Fundable originally charged 5% of the amount collected[15]. As of 9/13/2013, they were charging $99/month.

Table 7 lists deliverables Fundable suggests to be developed prior to the start of the fundraiser. Note that these are more geared toward investment fundraising than some other crowdfund sites.

Table 7: Fundable Suggested Deliverables (Investment Camp.)[16]

Deliverable	Purpose
Executive Summary	Brief overview of plan.
Fundraising Terms	Amounts to be raised and equity associate with investment
Business Plan	Marketing and strategic analysis
Pitch Deck	A brief pitch of the idea
Financials	Revenue and expense projections
Closing Documents	Legal documents to finalize equity agreement with Investor.

In 2014, as an extension of its investment class strategy, Fundable acquired LaunchRock. LaunchRock is a service that helps new startup businesses to find online followings and, eventually, customers. The service will continue to operate as a separate product from Fundable, but synergy for a startup (having both services from the same company) could be an opportunity they will be able to capitalize on in the near future[17]. Note that a service like LaunchRock would make a good tool for the pre-crowdfunding stage described earlier. In particular, it would be helpful for projects that may not have Kim and Eric's name recognition or pre-funding community foundation. LauchRock can also be thought of as a way to generate leads for Fundable.

Kickstarter

The Kickstarter name has become almost synonymous with crowdfunding. On April 28, 2009, Andy Baio, a Kickstarter board member and experienced technology entrepreneur, announced that the Kickstarter website had gone live[18]. Baio had already created the successful startup, Upcoming, which was a collaborative calendaring site that he sold to Yahoo in 2007. In 2008, he joined the board of Kickstarter.

In 2009, Baio described the Kickstarter mission by posting: "Kickstarter aims to let creative people of all kinds -- journalists, artists, musicians, game developers, entrepreneurs, bloggers -- raise money for their projects by connecting directly with fans, who receive exclusive access and rewards in exchange for their patronage."[19] It is interesting to note that while many tech startups choose to "pivot," or alter their mission for better focus, the Kickstarter direction has remained consistent. Today, the Kickstarter site lists a number of project types that are outside the scope of their mission and helps keep a creative or artistic focus.

For Kim and Eric, the Kickstarter focus seemed to be a good choice; however, as they moved into a new business phase of their careers, they decideded that the depth of business startup expertise and the ability to use the equity class of crowdfunding made Fundable a better choice. I also looked at Kickstarter as a place to fund publishing this book and found that the how-to business genre is not allowed under their book topic guidelines. Therefore, I found a better fit at Indiegogo.

In an ironic turn of events, Yahoo eventually chose to discontinue Baio's Upcoming site. In 2014, Baio launched a Kickstarter campaign to buy back the Upcoming domain name from Yahoo and relaunch the site.

Indiegogo

Indiegogo shows up in many lists as the second biggest of the crowdfunding sites. They describe themselves as international and allow for rewards fundraising on any topic, from small business to art projects. They also allow for cause or charity based crowdfunding. They do not have support for equity based crowdfunding.

Indiegogo launched in 2008.[20] Danae Ringelmann, Slava Rubin, and Eric Schell began the company in 2006 out of a shared frustration with the difficulty in raising money for film production and cancer research. They wanted to leverage Internet technology to get the word out and allow a large geographically dispersed group to pool their funds for a shared interest in a project. Danae's background was investment banking, and her personal frustration came from understanding the investment world and realizing it takes the right connections to a small number of individuals to go through channels in the banking world. Her vision was to bypass that system and democratize the fundraising model. Her personal story seems pretty cool in that she left investment banking and went to UC Berkley for her MBA for the purpose of starting a new crowdfunding venture.

In 2014, Indiegogo raised more than $40 million in new investment and included some stars in the business world as investors.[21] These investors clearly see Indiegogo positioned for major new growth. It will be interesting to watch where they go. The leaders have talked about moving into the equity side, but the site development efforts seem to focus on improving the rewards experience.

It is hard to say whether the industry is consolidating or fragmenting. The top few sites are becoming household names, while the technology to launch a crowdfunding platform is becoming much simpler by creating new specialized sites. Look for continued change in this industry as the technology simplifies and larger sites integrate better with other existing financial services, such as PayPal.

Chapter 2: Somewhere in Texas, Digitization Happens

In 1966, to the delight of his parents, Sylvia and Larry Stone, Eric Stone was born. Growing up in Corpus Christi and Beaumont, Texas, Eric's love for the Gulf was instilled at an early age, even before he embraced the guitar. Sylvia played guitar in a girl's band. Not professionally, as she described it, although still playing for audiences. She was excited to teach Eric guitar, but at first, he was too busy and focused on other interests. However, at age ten, Eric became sick and was stuck in bed at home for about six weeks which became a great time for Sylvia to teach him what she knew. She was amazed at how he took to playing guitar, teaching himself more and more until he was soon able to pass her own expertise. By junior high school, he had won his first contest playing guitar.

He practiced often and joined with high school friends to start a band (probably to meet chicks!). But in reality, Eric was on his way to writing his own music and becoming more adept at guitar although it would be some time before Eric would quit his day job[22]. Sylvia remembers his first band as a rock band that shook the house. He later started a country band. Sylvia remarked at the ease in which Eric could move between genres.

I wondered if Eric had gone to the same high school as Janis Joplin and maybe that would explain some of the creativity. He went to high school in Hamshire-Fanett, and she went about twenty miles away, in Port Arthur. However, they both studied in the sciences at Lamar University, so maybe some chemicals from science class spurred further musical experimentation for both of them.

Eric's first full-time job was that of tankerman, which consisted of transferring hazardous cargo to and from barges and ships. Finding a job at an airline, he moved from Texas to Florida and joined a new band in his off-time. There he continued to hone his stage presence and guitar licks. Later, he moved to Hawaii, added the ukulele to his repertoire, and took a serious turn for the tropical[23].

In one of Eric's podcasts, the interviewer noted how relaxed Eric was on stage and asked if he always found it easy to perform. Eric said, "No way." In fifth grade, he had to perform "Louisiana Saturday Night," by Mel McDaniel, and almost threw up (Stone, Eric Stone Radio, 2013). He had already been writing songs at that age but was new to performing.

While keeping his day job at Pitney Bowes, Eric was writing and performing during his off-time. He really wanted to work full-time on singing and songwriting to improve his craft. At a work conference in Atlanta, he told some of his colleagues about his dream to move to Nashville and hone his skills. They told him that there were openings in the Nashville office, and he should apply. Within a couple of weeks, he received the good news that he secured one of the openings. He packed the moving van and was off for a new adventure in Music City, USA (Stone, Eric Stone Radio, 2013).

In 1994, after his move to Nashville, he wanted to record an album and began researching his options. Most of the studios seemed intimidating and expensive to a new artist. He chanced upon an ad for Direct Image Studio that offered a reasonable price. He gave them a call and owner, Kenny Royster, answered the phone. Kenny didn't use any high-pressure tactics to get Eric to sign up for high-priced time, but rather, invited Eric in to listen to some sessions. Kenny had, and still has, a vision for helping the singer-songwriter community, no matter what level of fame and fortune the artists' careers are at the moment. Started just a few years before Eric moved to Nashville, the studio has now produced more than 8,000 songs.

Eric signed up with Kenny for an initial session and recorded three songs that wound up on his first CD release, *Songs for Sail*, in 1999. Eric describes working with Kenny in the studio as a dream. Kenny, in addition to running a great studio, is an excellent vocal coach and gives singer-songwriters tips that can really make their vocals pop. As Kenny assembles the right musicians for each song, the vocal coaching is sort of a free bonus. A nice result of Kenny's coaching is that Eric now does his own harmonies in the studio. On *Time to Fly*, all of the harmonies are Eric's voice. To hear more about the recording process that Eric follows at Direct Image Studio, listen to his Episode 1: *Time to Fly* podcast[24].

When "Songs for Sail" came out, Eric was looking for a way to market the CD and came up with the idea of playing it at boat shows. They are certainly full of people who have some of the same dreams and aspirations that you can find in Eric's music. Although social networking technology was nothing like it is today, the Internet was springing to life and Eric was able to look up the boat shows and email as many people as he could to try to get a gig.

In 1999, Eric was hired for a try-out at the Strictly Sail Chicago Boat Show[25] . While there, he met Bob Bitchin. The boat show promotion was a success, and as Eric was invited to many more, he developed a strong boat-show following. His work as a musician dovetailed nicely with Bob Bitchin's propensity to launch boating parties and a wonderful partnership began. The niche market became a great base island to launch the CD sales-leg of Eric's adventure. Eric warns, though, that while starting a niche may get you started with a group sharing a natural affinity for your work, you need to branch out into other niches, grow your music, and grow your community.

Steve Hall and Shelly Hero had been making music together since high school. Steve, with his sharp leads, and Shelly, with her rhythmic percussions (not to mention her sultry voice), made some great music across a number of genres, including music from Neil Young, Fleetwood Mac, and Judas Priest, just to name a few. They made their life in Florida, raised a daughter, and kept the beat. At the St. Petersburg Power and Sailboat Show in 1999, they watched Eric perform, enjoyed his music, and chatted him up while he broke down his equipment. Hitting it off, they kept in touch and later invited Eric back to their marina in Panama City, Florida, for a few drinks, a few chords, and some fun. At the time, Eric had been gigging solo in Destin, so he invited Steve and Shelly to join him there for six nights at Fudpuckers. The show went well, and the three piece set-up filled out Eric's sound nicely.

Eric then invited Steve and Shelly to play with him for a week in Antigua. Shelly said, "Absolutely," not really believing he'd pull it off. He did, and the band continued to play for one week out of every year for the next several years in a row. Eric has had, and continues to have, a great sense of band logistics. He must navigate not just getting a band and its equipment to a gig, but also setting up relationships, bartering to obtain a place for the band to stay, securing multiple gigs on the same general path, and setting up mini-tours, and eventually, bigger tours.

The Eric Stone Band then began expanding their tour schedule with great gigs in New Orleans, Canada, and the North East. Eric purchased a full-sized tour bus allowing him to bring the band and equipment on a wide-range of national tours. Shelly recalls that touring on the bus for extended amounts of time was always an adventure. She recalls that on one occasion, they took the tour bus to play some gigs in New York and were driving through the snow. Eric, at the wheel, found the exit, but while traveling down the exit ramp, they soon realized the tour bus was not going to fit under the overpass. Steve and Shelly were consigned to head outside, in shorts, to make sure Eric could back the bus back onto the highway. Quite a sight, but since traffic had backed-up behind them, it would have been hard to be sure if it was clear. Luckily, they continued on and made it to the gig.

The mainland tours were expanding, and word was starting to spread about this rising trop-rock musician, but the adventures really expanded with Bob Bitchin and Captain Woody. Having traveled the world on *SV Lost Soul* and having started the leading magazine by cruisers for cruisers, *Latitudes and Attitudes*, Bob Bitchin is the quintessential adventurer. Later, he founded the now-popular *Cruising Outpost* magazine. Captain Woody, also an accomplished circumnavigator with a book about the journey, now focuses on amazing group charter voyages with his organization, Adventure Voyaging. In group charters, Captain Woody reserves a number of sailboats in amazing locations, usually island oriented, and invites people to sign up for the available berths. Well, what would an island sailing adventure be without great island music? These adventures had become another exciting leg of Eric's adventures, allowing him to travel with the sailors, both captaining sailboats, and playing some of the venues in the ports visited by the flotilla. One cool sail adventure would be in Tonga, located in the South Pacific, and Eric, Steve, and Shell would have yet another musical experience.

Tonga is the place that makes you slow down and smell the rum. Their tag line is, "The True South Pacific." The Kingdom of Tonga is a group of over 170 islands that have not been conquered by foreign powers, and as such, have kept their unique and simple way of life. Tonga is ruled by a monarchy that has stood the test of time by governing its people in peace for more than a thousand years. The form of government is not unlike the monarchies of Europe that long ago tumbled. In part, this is because of its isolation, but perhaps, it is also because of the temperament of the ruling family and that the people there have found no need for revolution. Or just maybe, it's the beauty. Look out at the unique shades of blue and green in the sky and sea, see the greens of the naturally abundant palms, have a taste of the simply cooked fish, and you will see no reason to start a war. In May 2005, The Eric Stone Band made the pilgrimage to the Kingdom of Tonga!

The next day, Shelly and the others sat cross-legged in a circle, sharing a bowl of kava. Shelly confessed that the kava itself was not all it was cracked up to be but sharing ritual in paradise was still wonderful. The exciting part of the adventure came when they were able to play for the Prince of Tonga.

Once back in the mainland U.S., things were really getting busy on the tour schedule. At the height of touring, they would sometimes do three gigs in a day. Shelly recalls the crazy schedule with fondness.

Fanning the flames of the tour was Eric's prolific song-writing. Shelly said when Eric was writing *Long Boards and Short Stories* he must have written three or four songs in one day.

In 2008, Eric moved to the Virgin Islands and embarked on a busy local venue schedule, working six to seven nights a week and, at the same time, keeping with the boat shows and other events back on the U.S. mainland. A musician living in the Virgin Islands seems like a dream come true, and it is, but behind the scenes, the challenges of gigging on multiple islands can be interesting.

To play at different venues in the islands required Eric's 17' Edgewater center console powerboat instead of the typical tour bus that might have been used on the mainland. To move equipment, the boat had to be carefully packed to protect the equipment from sand, water, and the jarring of a sea passage. After docking the Edgewater at the closest dock to the venue, the equipment would still have to be hauled down the dock, sometimes across a sandy beach, and to the venue stage. At times, the sand and water may not have seemed like friendly companions, but when Eric got to play his original music for the fans who knew it, the day's work was put into perspective.

Around the 2011 time frame, stress from ending a bad relationship and the killer schedule did take its toll, and Eric was unable to write much new material or get back in the studio. The *Time to Fly* album was the result of Eric's new awakening, when he was ready to create again. The title came when Eric was preparing his Summer Tour Schedule and working up to the last minute before heading to the airport. He looked at his watch and said, "It's time to fly." It struck him with its dual meaning of literally time to head to the airport and also time to get the music, and his life, flying again. The concept, the album, and really, the next phase of Eric's life, took off. About the first song, Eric said, "'Time to Fly' is a commitment to living a full and happy life and achieving your goals and stuff like that."

What was Kim Up To?

Idaho may not be the expected start for cruisers, but Kim Hess was raised there in a small mountain community where she developed a love for family and the outdoors[26]. She loved both snow and water skiing in the area and started sailing in 1989. She began teaching as an aerobics instructor in 1992 and completed her Yoga teacher training in 2003.

In 2007, Kim published her book, *Yoga Onboard*, as well as a DVD by the same title, as a guide to keeping fit while cruising[27]. Kim had integrated her healthy yoga exercise with her love of sailing, recognizing the challenges of keeping fit while spending extended periods of time on a boat with limited space.

In 2009, Kim studied for and received her Captain's License or, more correctly, Merchant Marine Officer's License[28]. On November 20, 2009, Kim changed her ring tone to Lyle Lovett's "If I had a Boat,"[29] a pretty song. If you don't know the song, YouTube it before continuing. It sets the mood for Kim's section. She had just purchased and moved aboard a 41' Morgan Classic sailboat and had begun to prepare the boat and herself to charter with the Boy Scouts at Sea Base in Islamorada. She describes it as a leap of faith since she came from sailing a 21 footer. Hey, a sloop's a sloop, except for the engines and systems and how long it takes to come to a rest. She described how she had to come up to speed while learning to repair and maintain all of the boat systems. Hearing her describe getting to work on them made me feel guilty about not getting back to fixing my engine problems (maybe after this book is complete). Little did she know at the time, she would later rename the boat S/V, Ave de Paso, after Eric's song released on his *Time to Fly* album.

I asked Kim's good friend Liz (Elizabeth Rogerio) to send me some notes on those Miami years and here is her reply:

Back in 2005, I was a typical 'worker bee' living in a cubicle fifty   to sixty hours per week for a commercial real estate company on Brickell Avenue in downtown Miami. Like most average people, I was suffering from common ailments and stress associated with being confined to a sedentary workplace day after day. After a wise decision to take charge of my life and be more active, I joined a gym near my office. I picked up a schedule and noticed an evening yoga class at 7:00 pm. Being somewhat of a yoga novice, I was apprehensive at first. Some other previous yoga experiences included a Hatha session that consisted of a long 90 minutes of rhythmic breathing and another session where some overzealous, inexperienced yogis tried to twist me into a pretzel. While I'm sure that type of yoga is amazing and important, I needed to move and stretch my   body at manageable and sustainable pace. I like Kim's yoga class from the start. She stuck to the fundamentals of yoga but taught us to be playful and BREATHE. I never put much thought in my daily breathing. I still hear Kim in my head, "be conscious of your breath" and I find myself inhaling and exhaling with intention and purpose. I needed to get the blood flowing and relieve some stress and I did just that. Her yoga class not only got me stretching, moving and breathing better, but it launched a friendship spanning almost a decade (so far).

After that yoga class, Kim and I became fast friends. We met for lunch one day at the former Van Dyke Café on Lincoln Road on Miami Beach.

Conversation came very easy and we sat there for hours enjoying some killer Mojitos while talking about our lives, hopes, and dreams. It wasn't long before Kim introduced me to her dream of living on a sailboat and writing a book about incorporating a yoga practice into a live aboard cruiser lifestyle. I admired Kim from the very beginning. She has this infectious smile and oozes an entrepreneurial spirit. I had no doubt that it wouldn't be long before she'd make that dream a reality. Little did I know, I'd be able to witness and be a part of it.

In 2006, an apartment opened up in Kim's building on Miami Beach. At the time, I lived in bad part of downtown Miami and when this opening became available, my husband and I jumped at the chance to move to this nice area and become neighbors. Before we rented the Uhaul, Kim was already well on her way to looking at and purchasing a sailboat. She had begun brainstorming and developing a layout for her book. My husband Rodrigo had some Adobe software experience and a decent web design background, so it seemed fate took over the book started to materialize page by page. Over the course of several months, we'd have meetings around her large coffee table while sitting on pillows in the middle of her living room. Meetings would always include something yummy from her crockpot and were usually followed by "Killer Kim's Margaritas" (later to appear on the Dockside menu) or just some great tequila on the rocks. It didn't take long before Kim was shooting the Yoga Onboard DVD in Tampa and sending the final   book to the printer. I remember celebrating "compound style" as we called it around a campfire in our front yard. We opened a magnum of champagne and toasted to her dream becoming a reality.

Once the boxes of Yoga Onboard books arrived, Kim was traveling a lot going to boat shows around the country. It was at the Miami Boat show that I met Eric Stone for the first time. I knew from the moment I met Eric that he and Kim seemed to have a lot in common and shared that same entrepreneurial spirit. Fast forward several years later, Kim owns and lives on a boat in Islamorada; she's married to Eric Stone, she's a business owner and a yoga instructor. She made everything we talked about years earlier happen. So why stop there?

Being a fan of the former Dockside Bar and Grill at Sombrero Marina in Marathon, Florida, I was sad to hear when it closed down. I no longer had a place to stop in to get a beer on my way down to Key West. Off and on I would swing by and visit Kim and Eric in Islamorada on my way down US1 or would travel down on a Saturday night just to see the Eric Stone Band play at Salty's, Snapper's or Smuggler's Cove. When Kim and Eric shared their intentions of taking over Dockside, I thought it was a genius plan. I could not think of two better people who share the same vision who would undoubtedly revitalize this establishment into nothing short of amazing. I didn't even know crowdfunding existed until I saw Eric post the Fundable link on Facebook. I was a bit skeptical at first and was not sure the kind of reception they'd receive using this unfamiliar online tool. Of course with Eric and Kim's followers and support network, they were able to spread the word

and raise an impressive amount of money to launch
the first phase of improvements which would
ultimately lead to the grand reopening of Dockside
Tropical Café.

The Digital Era Begins

During the same years when Eric was honing his chops and beginning what would become a prolific recording career, the world of digital media was exploding. The commercial compact disk (CD), released in 1982 (Wikipedia), introduced music to digital technology but maintained the old business model for music. While the grooved vinyl platter gave way to laser-read bits on a shiny reflective surface, nothing much else changed for the moment. In-between, multiple formats of magnetic tape, while bemoaned by audiophiles, introduced a higher level of portability to music.

Digital technology converted the continuous audio waveform to a sequence of bits, binary digits, ones, and zeros. The technology that allowed audio and video to be converted to bits and bytes is called "sampling." Sampling is simply measuring the amplitude of the sound or video at a particular time and recording its value as a number. In doing so, a song becomes a series of numbers which are then easy for computers to manipulate and transfer. In one sense, it may seem that measuring a sound or video at particular discrete intervals might lead to a choppy or uneven playback, but it is the high rate of sampling that makes the choppiness undetectable by people's ears and eyes. For example, music CDs usually have over 44 thousand samples per second on each of the stereo channels. For each of those sampling intervals, a 16-bit number is recorded, allowing for nearly 65 thousand levels of measurement. A full length CD with seventy minutes of music would take about 600 million (or mega) bytes of data. That was a lot of data in the old days, but new computers and fast networks can manipulate that amount of data with no problem, bringing with it fairly inexpensive high quality A/V devices, like the Apple iPod/iPhone product lines.

Meanwhile, an arcane technology developed during the Cold War allowed very different computers to be interconnected easily. While the networks connecting computers have been around nearly as long as computers, they were custom-designed and managed individually. One of the very interesting aspects of this particular technology that came to be called the "Net" was the use of common standards and, in particular, open protocols for communication. This enabled many different vendors to develop technologies based on these open standards. Competition reduced the cost of these devices and made them more affordable, leading to rapid growth. The 80's saw the communication protocols converge on the TCP/IP networking technologies, so most networks could talk to each other, opening up the public Internet as we now know it.

The Internet itself was really just the connection between computers. So what do you do with computers that are interconnected? We have an early answer for that. Back in the early 1970's, when the DoD still managed the net (ARPANET), a study was done on net usage. This study found that the first "killer-app" was something that tied together a file transfer program and a text editor. We know it now as e-mail. Another part of the study showed that most e-mail traffic between the scientists and engineers who used e-mail (and you had to be a certified scientist to get on the net in those days) was trivial, marginal stuff – what we would classify as gossip! The more technology changes, the more human behavior brings us back to our inner caveman! Another net application that was developed in 1989 was the World-Wide Web (Web), which brought the technology to the masses. Well, not immediately, but definitely the skills needed to use the web were far from that needed to be a rocket scientist. In effect, this brought the net down from the halls of academe to the marketplace, making it more accessible to all of us. Around the same time, legislation made it possible to use the net for commercial purposes since its predecessor, the Arpanet, was limited to government and research.

The original Web, sometimes called Web 1.0, is fairly simple technology. A Web host stores a page on its disk drive or other storage device. A Web browser on a user's computer requests the page, and after receiving it, displays it on the user's screen. The data for the request and the page sent back goes through the network of computers, or the Internet. So how do web pages that are developed independently all show up on your browser? The pages are tagged in HTML, one of the many open standards on the net, which make it a global system. The first version of HTML was invented by Tim Berners-Lee and released publicly in 1991. Tim reportedly wanted a way to share documents over the CERN network and developed HTML, a language to describe documents, based on an older SGML standard. Essentially, the approach permitted two things. First, it allowed each document on an inter-connected system, with many different computers, to be accessed easily; second, it had a hyperlink to click on a link and gain access to a remote document. The first feature gave each document a unique locater (URL), and the second provided a hyper-link, which gave rise to "surfing the web." Finally, someone without any computer-coding skills could work their way through a global library of documents.

That was all well and good, but merely reading a document did not support a transaction, which is the exchange of money essential to commerce. Many of these features were bolted onto the net's architecture. The addition of databases and multimedia are sometimes called Web 2.0. Businesses offered search features on their websites to support users in finding a product that matched their requirements. Forms were developed to submit data, including payment information, to a remote database. Documents for websites were generated on the fly by a computer program that used data in a database rather than custom coding each page for each user. One problem, a holdover from the early days of the commercial net, was that many users still perceived anything on the net as a free good. This goes back to the first few decades in the net's history, when the net was maintained for scientific and research use and things on the net were free! Commercial businesses found it difficult to turn a profit on the net. For a short time, during the dot-com boom of 1998-2000, they even claimed that losing money was good since it meant they were growing. Reality sunk in with the dot-com bust, though the sky-high valuation of net companies still leaves room for caution and the need for a healthy dose of common sense.

One other technology of special relevance to the music industry, and Eric's first business, is a compression technology that reduces file sizes on the net. We talked about digitization, the process of converting a continuous waveform, such as sound, into a set of zeros and ones. Typically, that results in a large file. A compression technique that reduces audio file size, an MP3, was developed in Germany, with software for the conversion released by the Fraunhofer society on July 7, 1994. The convergence of a slew of technologies hit the music industry in the following years. The net provided a globally inter-connected file network. Digital media players allowed users to carry their music with them. MP3 digitized the music into small, portable files. Finally, the bulk of new music lovers – young people – were the most savvy with this new technology. It was indeed a perfect storm for the established music business. Later in this book, as we deal with crowdfunding and the convergence of social network, the net, mobile devices, and virtual communities, we will consider whether crowdfunding is going to be a game changer, like digital music, or a bit-player in the technology bandwagon.

Here is another example of the changes brought about by Web 2.0: when you write a post on Facebook, you have added value to the community on Facebook. Note, that unlike Web 1.0, the major source of value is not the page created by the company; the major source of value in Web 2.0 is the posts of the community. The value of the Web 2.0 provider arises from its size, the result of the number of users contributing to the site, and the organization and presentation of user contributed content by the site. The first source of value is impacted by the network effect, which is the increase in value of a technology as more people use it. Consider a telephone. If there is only one, it has no value. If two people have phones, then it becomes more valuable. If ten people in the community have phones, the value increases further. When most people in the community have phones, those without phones are on the losing side of the digital divide. The second value of the web 2.0 site is the way in which it organizes and presents the data. To over simplify, Facebook works by writing the status you type into the status line of your page to a database. Then when your "friend" logs in, the status along with your friend's other friend's status message are read from the database, sorted, and displayed in the news feed. Of course, the algorithm Facebook uses to select messages and prioritize them has become increasingly sophisticated over the years.

Web 2.0, like Web 1.0 earlier, has its successes and failures. One particular value of Web 2.0 is the ability to create an online community. Online communities are not new to the net. The Well[30], launched in 1985, enjoyed a significant following among net denizens of that era. In particular, due to its ability to span geographic and political boundaries, while offering a voice to a vast number of individuals, Web 2.0 provides the ability for small focused groups to congregate, communicate, transact, and sustain themselves online. It is this feature of Web 2.0 that we will see in crowdfunding: the ability to nurture and cultivate an online group for a purpose.

So these three things – digital content, the Internet, and Web 2.0 – open up the world to individuals and small organizations to create high quality content and distribute it widely. Of course, much of the content that is developed may not be considered high quality. While the openness of the web allows anybody to post content, most of the content is in the words of Sir Walter Scott, "unwept, unhonoured, unsung." However, the technical quality of web postings has increased over time. Better equipment and the need to rise from the mass of posted content makes it necessary to produce content of (at least) higher technical quality. Have you browsed YouTube lately? Kenny Royster, Eric's studio guy, notes the increase in sonic quality between 1994, when Eric did his first album, and 2013, when *Time to Fly* came out. Kenny says he had upgraded the studio forty times in the intervening years to get to what is now world class sound (Stone,

Episode 4, Interview with Kenny Royster, 2013). Professional production still needs skill and experience, though much of the process is considerably less expensive and more accessible than in the past. The same is true of a crowdfunding proposal. The communication must be professionally managed to rise above the higher threshold set in the marketplace.

Chapter 3: Social Networking Technology as a Platform

Although crowdfunding technology allows your fans to contribute to your project, getting the word out and keeping fans informed requires harnessing a number of technologies into a social networking platform. The traditional webpage is often still the anchor of an electronic presence, while newer sites, like Facebook, allow for much greater interaction. As was described earlier with Eric and Kim's crowdfund, the Fundable site provided a place for fans to contribute, but Eric and Kim made extensive use of email and Facebook to keep fans updated on the status of the project and a web page that defined their concept. It is the use of a set of mutually reinforcing technologies that makes for a successful social networking platform.

Today, the web page, with an easy to remember domain name that can be publicized, and links to all of your other tools, still remains an anchor for your social networking platform. The blog built on the webpage makes it easy to write new articles to your webpage with more current information. Web and blog technology have merged because many use the same technology for both, as you will see in more detail below. Email lists still play a role since they can send your newsletter to your fans' inbox where it won't be lost as easily as the new Facebook and Facebook-like technologies. Micro-blogging encompasses all of the fast-paced, short message services, like Facebook, Twitter, and Instagram.

This chapter explores social networking technologies, where they came from, and how to use them as tools within an integrated framework. The chapter begins with the webpage and some basics about the Internet just to give you some background about where the technologies came from and how they work. Mailing lists and mailing list management software follows, and the microblogs will be introduced and described at the end. This section is sort of a catchall with lots of little related tidbits, like domain names, picture and video formats, and some mention of the major underlying technologies.

There are many ways to implement and use these technologies. This book takes the perspective of a professional, individual, or small business person who would like to implement some of these technologies themselves but is not looking to be a computer scientist. So some techno-geek details are given, but easy implementation strategies are recommended.

Web Sites

Your webpage resides on a web server. When you write a text page and post it on the web server, it is tagged with HTML to render on different web browsers. A person looking for your site enters your domain name, and the browser software asks the server for the page. There is some work done in the plumbing of the net to get the request from the user's browser to the webserver, and back, but that is typically transparent to the user. Unless, of course, the webpage does not exist on the server and the 404 (page not found) error shows up, or the webserver goes down and a 500 (internal server error) is displayed. What makes it a little complicated is that if you want a cool multimedia look and feel, or if you want the site to be interactive and allow users to send you information or make purchases, the web page will have a lot of computer code in the file. You can write that code by hand (yuck), use web page editing software (more fun), or choose a hosting site with standard templates that bundled all these features in an easy to use web page (super fun and easy). In the past, hosted web templates created dull and boring websites while custom coded sites allowed richly interactive sites. That is no longer true. In fact, unless you have a clear business reason, there is no need to use anything other than a standard template. Website developers typically try to upsell their services and present the following arguments in favor of custom developed sites:

(i) The site will be branded for your business, creating a unique impact rather than a cookie cutter look and feel of templates.

(ii) Custom security features can be built into the site.

(iii) The unique business processes of your company warrant a custom site.

Here are the problems with these arguments. Branding has nothing to do with custom site design. Use your corporate color theme, logo, and unique message and images on a template. Your site is unique. What do you get by keeping your margin at 38 pixels instead of 36? In fact, since customers develop skills in traversing multiple sites on the web, they will find your site confusing if it is, indeed, very different. On the other hand, users have no problems with a template that is widely used. In fact, high usability is often the reason a template is widely used. In addition, with the wide diversity of user devices for browsing, ranging from full size displays to small portable smartphones, templates are designed to render effectively on all devices, solving another problem for your business website. Visit the site webbyawards.com, the Oscars of web design. Look at the site winners from ten years ago. How many of these companies are successful online ventures today? Look at the supersites on the web – Amazon, eBay, Facebook – and their design. Clean, uncluttered, and functional. Flying monkeys and rich graphics don't drive business to your site. In fact, boo.com, one of the notorious flameouts in the dot-com boom-bust, floundered due to rich graphics.

The second argument is flat-out wrong. The safest site, or software, is one that is tried and tested. It is when new programming is done that security holes open up. In coding, one rule is clear: every feature is a potential bug. The best security is to use a mature product that is widely used. Even if there is a problem, it will be fixed soon since the product is widely used.

If you are developing the next Facebook or eBay, then OK. Otherwise, your business model has good templates for its website.

The only reason you might not use the template is if you are in the web programming business and are creating new ways for pages to work. A javascript coder might build a unique website to demonstrate cutting edge javascript programming skills like the kind that enabled young Mr. Zuckerberg to make a mark on the Harvard social scene by creating Facebook. Another is, of course, if you take a college course with us, where we require you to custom code a website! Ah, the joys of higher education.

Since a web page is just a file on a computer called a web server, you need to be able to make the file and put it on the server. The file is written in its own language called hypertext markup language (HTML). The original version of this language was invented by Tim Berners-Lee in 1992[31]. He wanted a simple way to mark up documents so they would be easy to share on the web. Chapter 2 of *Raggett on HTML 4* is available free online and has a nice little history of HTML, if you are looking for more[32]. Since the invention of the original HTML, other languages have been added to the mix to enhance what the document could do. For example, cascading style sheets (CSS) provide a way to change the formatting of a webpage and can allow the formatting to be used consistently across a set of pages. DFO it once and use it many times. Both HTML and CSS languages are now updated and improved by the World Wide Web Consortium (W3C). The W3C homepage provides great tutorials and references on the languages if you want to get into the nitty gritty[33].

Of course if you don't want to learn those languages, you can use an HTML editor. The HTML editor will let you edit a document, like using a word processor, but the file will be saved in the html language. Microsoft Word can even be used by selecting "Save As" to save a document in html format. One problem with Word, and why we would never recommend using MS-Word to create a webpage, is the massive amount of bloat in the HTML page created by Word. Many serious web designers use the editors and then go in and tweak the code, so knowing html is still useful. There are many packages out there, but Adobe Dreamweaver and Microsoft Visual Studio are a couple of the big names.

If you make your own pages, either by hand coding them in html or using a html editor, you will need to transfer them to a web server, often called publishing, for them be seen by the public. There are a number of sites to pick from, and it may be hard to decide which one is best. If you have a friend that does something similar, you might go along with his or her choice because whatever site you pick, it is good to have somebody to talk with about how it is working (or not working) from time to time.

The site you choose is not etched in stone, but eventually, it will be harder and harder to change. When you are beginning with minimal content, you can change to another provider fairly easy. Eventually, you will have a lot of content, and some will be formatted to best fit the one provider. So feel free to dive in and get started, but realize your first choice probably will not be your last and that your second or third choice will become more permanent.

Sample Hosting Sites
Weebly
Wix
Azure
Bluehost
Webs
Plebu
Site5.com
Go Daddy

Search Engine Optimization (SEO)

A long time ago, SEO meant spending a lot of time with your keyword meta tag (a tag within your web page that is not displayed to the reader but was picked up by search engines). Since search engines were reading that, and web designers knew it, the web designers would put words related to their site in there just to attract hits. Since early search engines used simplistic rules, one common approach was to merely repaste a word hundreds or even thousands of times on the home page to move up the search rankings. Search engine designers didn't think that was useful, so they stopped ranking sites based on the keyword meta tags[34]. Google's algorithm started out by looking at page links, and at inward page links in particular. The logic was that if a site was good, many other sites would link to it. Hence, inward page links were seen as an indicator of site quality, and hence, organic search engine ranking. This led to site farms, where people generated sites purely for the purpose of creating links to other sites and boosting their SEO status (for a small fee, of course). As Google improved its algorithm, SEO techniques kept pace. In one sense, SEO is a little like an arms race. If you do something to improve your site ranking, your competition will likely notice and copy it. In addition, people continually game the search engine ranking algorithm to boost their own ranking, while search engine designers work continually to ferret out these techniques and re-organize their organic search results to be "true." So, to some extent, it is a moving target. Of course, the good old-fashioned approach of developing and posting useful content still helps.

Once a search engine finds a bunch of pages related to a person's search, it displays them on the screen for the searcher to pick what they want to look at. The little blurb written is called the "title and snippet," and usually gets its information from the page's title tag and description meta tag. By making those tags relevant and interesting, you display your link on the search engine page in its best light for the human part of the system where the reader now has to decide to click the link. Note that merely gaining SEO rank does not help. If you have a business servicing transmissions, and your SEO boosts you for the keyword "transmission repair," it is helpful. However, if your business has one garage in New Orleans, does it help to be on page one in Florida? It is more important to rank high among potential customers rather than across the WWW.

Web page editing tools can help you edit those tags without knowing the html codes. For the geeks that want to see the HTML code, it is shown in Figure 7.

<title>Kenneth R. Walsh, Information Systems Associate Professor, University of New Orleans</title>
<meta name="description" content="Kenneth R. Walsh, Information Systems Associate Professor, University of New Orleans. Classes and research summarized. Local IT links.">

Figure 7: Title and Meta Description Tags

Keep reading:
http://googlewebmastercentral.blogspot.com/2012/06/seo-essentials-for-startups-in-under-10.html

Domain Names

A domain name is the name we use to refer to a site on the web. For example, Facebook.com is the domain name of the Facebook site. All sites on the Internet need unique names so that when you type that name into the browser, there is only one unique destination. Technically, computers talk to each other using IP addresses, but those are numbers rather than words, so the domain name gives a more human name for the site. In reality, the browser converts the domain name to an IP address before the computers start talking to each other.

Eric and Kim chose docksidetropicalcafe.com for the domain name for their venue.

We chose tropnetworking.com for the book. We also purchased tropnetworking.org, tropnetworking.net, and tropnetworking.info so as to clear up confusion from another organization using those domain names for their sites. The extra domain names may have been overkill, but we were on a roll that day.

Of course, your new domain name must be unique, so you need to check if that name you covet has already been taken. Search the Internet for a domain name provider, and they will let you type in potential domain names and show you if they are taken or available. There is a charge for domain name registration, and it can be more convenient to register your domain name from the same provider as your web page. See the next section on how to choose a web site provider before spending the money.

Blog

What is a blog?

A blog, short for we**b log**, is way to post longer, more permanent commentary to a page. The entries are longer than those usually posted on social networks, like Facebook, and will stay at the same location overtime rather than being fleeting, like on a news feed. However, you will need to ask your readers to take a look at them. While really simple syndication (RSS) was designed to get people to subscribe to blogs, the technology failed to gather the momentum to become mainstream on the net. A facebook post or tweet can link to a blog, offering the reader a link to a more detailed comment on a topic.

Blogs began in the mid-1990's, but by the end of the decade, experienced rapid growth. Around 1999, the Web Log moniker became shortened to blog, and people who wrote blogs became known as bloggers. In the early days, bloggers needed to know HTML, the language of the Web page, to create and post blogs. By the end of the 1990's, blog tools began to emerge, and so did an array of bloggers, many with less technical backgrounds (Blood, 2000).

A blog page is typically structured as a main page containing the blog posts that are typically displayed in reverse chronological order. A menu may allow the reader to select posts based on keywords, popularity, or other criteria. Readers are invited to post their own comments in response to the main post. Those comments can be either moderated or not. Moderated comments allow the blog owner to decide if the comments should go public or not before they are seen. In addition to preventing comments that vilify people or ideas, and/or use intemperate language, or advertise unrelated products, moderation establishes blog owners' control over their sites. In either case, the owner would have "delete-authority" over comments.

One blogger can even comment on their own blog about another blog. On my blog, I may tell you the best way to create a web page. However, my fellow web page designer may think she has a better way and may write a reply, but rather than post a comment to my blog (which I control), she may post it to her blog but reference my blog with either a trackback or pingback. Now she has control of her comment, which may be embedded in her blog about web design, and can reference my blog to explain her artistic difference. The trackback, or pingback, will show up in the comments of my management panel where I can choose whether to accept them in a similar way that allows me to moderate regular comments. Note that both sites have to enable their trackback and pingback options in order to communicate in this way. In a sense, the blog is one of the earliest social networking tools on the web.

In the early days of the net, a bohemian atmosphere prevailed in discussion forums, and blog comments were perceived as offering rich commentary on the topic that enhanced the message. In addition, anonymity encouraged commenters to express their opinions freely. While free speech is treasured in the U.S., blog managers can be held liable for comments in other countries, and a global business needs to monitor blog comments carefully. In addition, blog comments face a serious risk of comment spam when unregistered users are permitted to post comments. One common type of comment spam involves comments that have no relevance to the primary blog item but are used to promote a completely different product or service. Obviously, while user comments are valuable, we do not want to promote the next miracle herbal cure for every known ailment or the way to possess a dictator's hidden millions.

One of the good things about a blog is that, being permanently open to the public on the web, like a web page, it can garner search engine traffic. The search engine may send new readers to your site. Further, since others can comment, the content is expanding by more than just the things you have written. Integrating different voices, as compared to what could happen if you just wrote articles on a standard web page, is a good way to get your community to interact. Note that being "open to the public" on the web is easier for search engines to find than content with a particular system, such as Facebook. All content is seen by the search engine and all content can be read by readers without a login. (Note that a company could install a blog behind its intranet or firewall to create an internal company blog, but that is not the focus here.)

Why blog?

Blogging is a good way to provide more long-lasting advice to your community and, hopefully, extend your following by writing informative blogs that attract new readers.

A good blog will be one that matches the interests of your community with the particular skills that you have which could benefit your community. In general, we stick to general skills or topics, which will help your readers, rather than the particulars of your organization so that you can highlight your areas of expertise without selling. Those interested in your product can then follow through to your web page to see your offerings, and they are likely to be better informed having come through your blog.

To find the best blog hosting site, I typed "best blog hosting site" into Google search. Two problems struck me right away. Since "Top 10" or "Best" are typical things people look for, lots of sites are named with those words. There are, "Top Ten Websites," "Top Ten Blogs Sites," and even, "The Top Ten Weirdest Dinosaur Extinction Ideas."[35] One site with the title, "Top Ten Blog Sites," was completely blank. Many of the sites list examples that are popular just to attract search engines but have no real site content and no real methodology for selection.

Pingdom (2012) looked at the blog platform used by the top 100 blog sites, repeated their study in 2009 and 2012, and gave some good information on where the market is and how markets like this change over time. In both years, WordPress was ranked number 1, and in 2012, WordPress had 48% of this market. WordPress is clearly the dominant player and would like to remain a big player. The top ten platforms for 2009 are shown in Table 8, and the top ten platforms for 2012 are shown in Table 9. Typepad, 2009's number 2, dropped substantially to 2012's number 8. Note that the item labeled "custom" refers to blogs that have built their blog site using web tools and databases.

Table 8: 2009 Top 10 Blogging Platforms Based (Pingdom Study)

Rank	Blog Platform	Market Share of Top 100 Blog SItes
1.	WordPress	32%
2.	Typepad	16%
3.	Blogsmith	14%
4.	Moveable Type	12%
5.	Gawker	8%
6.	custom site	8%
7.	Drupal	7%
8.	Blogger	3%
9.	Express Engine	1%
10.	Scoop	1%

Table 9: 2012 Top 10 Blogging Platforms Based (Pingdom Study)

Rank	Blog Platform	Market Share of Top 100 Blog Sites
1.	WordPress	48%
2.	custom site	14%
3.	Moveable Type	7%
4.	Drupal	6%
5.	Gawker	5%
6.	Blogsmith	4%
7.	TypePad	2%
8.	Blogger	2%
9.	Scoop	1%
10.	Tumblr	1%

It is interesting to note that the use of custom tools to design a web site increased from 8% to 14% in a three year period. This approach may be favorable for larger companies with a vested interest in their blog because it can allow for better integration with other web site features or software that the organization uses. Development of custom blogs is not insurmountable by a web programmer. At its essence, it requires storing the comments to a relational database and retrieving them in an organized way for display. That said, the devil is in the details, and this will not be elaborated upon here. We will focus on making the best use of other people's work in other blog platforms.

We decided that since it was hard to find a definitive report on the best blog platform, we would try a bunch and see how they worked; thus we launched the "Blog Platform Smackdown." The same content about picking a blog platform was uploaded to each of the top blog sites identified in searching the web for recommendations. We did modify the Pingdom list to some extent. Drupal – which has a library of tools for developers to use and is really an alternative way of doing the custom blog – was eliminated since we were looking at platforms for non-programmers. Gawker was eliminated also because it is a blog itself for several bloggers rather than an open blogging platform for the public.

Tumblr falls in the micro-blog category, which is considered later in the book.

We narrowed our list to seven (all but Posthaven) supported basic blog features, including:

- Photos and video in posts
- HTML editing of posts
- Multiple authors
- Templates
- Customization of templates (administrator panel or editing of CSS and HTML files)
- Third Party Add-ons
- eMail Posting

As of October, 2013, Posthaven does not support video upload, html editing, multiple authors, and templates. Posthaven is a special case, and some experienced bloggers developed the platform on a mission to create a blog that will last forever. They have been included here because of their cool story, but we will have to see when features become available to make their blog fully operational.

Blogger

"Blogger was started by a tiny company in San Francisco called Pyra Labs in August of 1999."[36] Not liking the farming lifestyle, Evan Williams moved from Nebraska to near San Francisco to become a technology writer for O'reilly[37]. Later, enthralled with startups in the area, he moved closer to San Francisco and began the development of Blogger. Blogger was acquired by Google in 2002, and Evan made millions. Evan brought his team to Google but left what had become a corporate job.

Templates: Limited number

Cost: Free

Share buttons: email, Blogger, Twitter, Facebook, G+

Site URL: https://www.blogger.com/

Tropnetworking URL: http://tropnetworking.blogspot.com/

When setting up a Google Blogger account, you must have a google account. If you set up a Google account under your own name, then you can choose whether to use that personal account information as the identity of the blogger, or you can choose a blogging pseudonym that will be used with all of your posts. We set up the tropnetworking blog as a pseudonym under my gmail account. Gmail then allows the blog sub domain to be specified. The domain name for all google blogs is blogspot.com. We selected the subdomain tropnetworking and set up tropnetworking.blogspot.com.

Drupal

Drupal is an open source web page development platform that can be installed at a web service provider. The system provides an extensive lego-like set of modules that can be put together in an amazing number of configurations, including basic web page designs and blogs. We would classify this is a set of tools for web programmers rather than a blog or web platform, and would consider it a good way to do a completely new type of collaboration but not an easy way to get your blog published. Drupal was developed from the message board software developed in 1999 by Dries Buytaert[38].

Movable Type and Type Pad

Movable Type is blogging software that was written by then unemployed Ben Trott because his wife, Mena, wanted to blog[39]. (Hey, if you were unemployed and your wife wanted to blog, you would get to work too! Uh, er, maybe look for a job.) The software was originally sold for installation on your own site, but through mergers and acquisitions, as well as changes in strategy, the Type Pad hosted solution evolved. True to Ben's original hope, the site focuses on good support for customers and offers a premium level customer support at the $14.95/ month level. The Movable Type software starts at $595.00 for a 5 user license.

In October 2013, Movable Type released version 6 and a new plugin and theme libraries. The number of themes and libraries is much less than WordPress, but this release marks a serious new attempt to regain market share.

Posthaven

Posthaven was created by Gary Tan and Brett Gibson in 2013 after Twitter acquired, and subsequently shutdown, their last blog platform, Posterious. Posterious was launched in 2008 and was acquired by Twitter in 2012. After declining usage, Twitter announced that Posterious would close on April 30, 2013. Tan and Gibson were angry at all the lost opportunity, for letting the site decline, and the lost content following site demise. Twitter did give a warning window to users to export their content so they could save it or post it elsewhere.

The site is unique in that its mission grew out of the founder's anger at the decline of their former platform. They are creating a self-sustaining business model that will ensure the platform will be available forever. Although a pretty broad statement, the founders have been in the business for a considerable amount of time and understand what their claim entails. The pricing model is set at $5 per month with no free option. The idea of not having a free option, which is so common today, is that for the site to be truly sustainable by whatever blog community adopts it, it will need a steady cash flow that everybody should participate in. They also pledge to never have ads and to not seek investors. Investors often need to move their money out of a project at some point, usually selling to another investor or company. The transition can change the strategy of the organization. Further, their commitment to content that will be around forever even remains after the user cancels his or her account. If a user keeps his or her account current for one year, Gary and Brett promise to keep the content alive although without, obviously, editing privileges.

The pledge on their homepage says, "We'll never get acquired. We'll never shut down. You pay. We keep the lights on." A nice promise in this day and age of throw away electronics and media. Comments on LifeHacker show some mixed feeling as to whether Gary, co-founder of posterious, was involved with the sale to Twitter. Gary posted that he had already left the company. His post says, "The acquisition was about money. Posthaven is all about love."[40]

Have you ever completed a project and wished you could start over and do it again once you learned a number of ways to do it better? Gary and Brett were able to do just that. The software for PostHaven is being developed from scratch by Gary and Brett themselves, and having done this before with more primitive technology, I am sure they will have a much clearer vision of the architecture for their new product. I would bet that this approach would lead to very high-quality, reliable software and will eventually lead to some innovative new twists on the features. The downside of this approach is that a lot of work will need to be done just to include the most common features, and it will take some time to add new items. At our last inspection of the site on September 18, 2013, just the basic posting features were available.

Templates: Not yet

Cost: $5/ month

Share buttons: Twitter, Facebook

Site URL: https://posthaven.com/

Tropnetworking URL: http://tropnetworking.posthaven.com/

First impression: An interesting startup that we should watch. It does not yet have all the bells and whistles, but it does have an experienced startup team.

SquareSpace

SquareSpace makes its mark with a "less is more" approach to combining blogging and eCommerce. *Less* meaning less technical skill is needed to select and use templates that are simple but elegant in design. The general layout is that of a blog, but an eCommerce module is available to make the blog into a storefront.

Squarespace is an integrated web site, blog, and ecommerce platform that is offered as a service. The company was created in 2004 by Anthony Casalena. Squarespace defines itself as focusing a "fusion of design and engineering" (Squarespace, 2013, about page). The cool look and feel does give the impression of being less techy than the others.

Cost: $8/ month introduction; $16/ month unlimited blog and web; $24/ month with eCommerce

Tumblr

Tumblr falls in the microblogger category with short posts usually emphasizing picture attachments. David Karp started developing Tumblr in 2006 and launched in 2007. In 2013, Yahoo purchased Tumblr amongst protest by users who feared the freewheeling site would become too corporate. At this point, Yahoo has let Tumblr continue its course. We will have to wait and see what happens next.

The advertising model used on Tumblr is simpler than other sites in that there is not a separate posting method and advertising method. The same type of site is set up by the individual as a company, and a company can drive traffic by posting multimedia content and seeking followers. Followers are asymmetric, like Twitter.

Conversations are promoted with notes and likes to posts.

WordPress

WordPress was started in 2003 by Matt Mullenweg. Matt forked[41] the b2/café blogging software to continue upgrades as the original developers had appeared to discontinue development.[42] The b2/café software was an open source platform, free to use and modify, which gave way to the open nature of the WordPress product today. The software is still free to download. By 2012, WordPress powered 70 million sites.[43] Maybe more important, a 2012 study found that 48% of top 100 blog sites were powered by WordPress.[44]

Word Press sites can be created either at Wordpress.com or at many web page hosting sites. A web hosting site can use Wordpress simply by downloading the Wordpress software to a folder on the site. The features are nearly the same in either location; however, the cost is just for the hosting, so it will vary by the hosting company.

The strength of WordPress is its long term popularity and open source design. Many people and organizations have developed templates for WordPress, making for a wide variety of choices rich with customization options.

Templates: Many

Site URL: http://wordpress.com/ (for hosted by WordPress sites.)

Tropnetworking URL: http://tropnetworking.wordpress.com/

To use the WordPress software at another web hosting site, the software will need to be uploaded to the site. Many web hosting sites already support WordPress, so adding WebPress features may just meaning clicking a button on the hosting site to add the features. If the site does not provide support, then the software can be manually uploaded to one of your web folders.

Which Blog Platform is Best for You?

The TropNetworking BlogSmackdown compared seven blog platforms, including Blogger, Movable Type, Posthaven, Squarepage, Type Pad, WordPress.com, and WordPress.org. The costs at the time we looked at the platforms are summarized in Table 10 and some additional features are listed in Table 11. The best blog platform depends on how you plan to use the blog, but the huge market share and vital development community around WordPress are going to make those options a top choice for many. Both of those platforms also support standard webpages and make a good platform for your web page as well, making it easy to integrate the two. Interestingly, custom blogs were the second most popular alternative in the Pingdom study. Custom blogs can be good for larger companies or high tech companies with the skills to set up the databases and the link to the page, but they do take more work than most companies would want to put in. The added work can, however, make a blog that is well integrated with other systems in the organization.

Table 10: Blog Costs

Site	Initial Site	Custom Domain	Unlimited Storage	Unl. Blog
Blogger	Free	Yes*	Unlimited posts	100
Movable Type	$8.95/mon.	Inc.	Inc.	$14.95
PostHaven	$5/mon.	Inc.	Unlimited posts	10
Squarespace	$8/mon.	Inc	$16/mon.	$8 for 20; $16 for unlimited
Type Pad	$8.95-$49.95/ mon.	Yes	Yes	Yes (at $14.95 and above)
Wordpress.com (hosted)	Free	$13-$18/ year	Yes	Yes
WordPress.org @godaddy	Free	Yes*	Supported by host web provider	Supported by hosting provider

*Purchase domain name elsewhere.

Table 11: Blog Features

Site	Priority Support	MailChimp Integration	eCommerce
Blogger	no	no	no
Movable Type	$29.95	no	Plugins
PostHaven	no	no	no
Squarespace	no	Inc w/16$/month	$24/month
Type Pad	Yes (at $29.95 and above)	Embedded form	No
Wordpress.com (hosted)	Yes	Embedded form	Partner Store Fronts
WordPress.org @godaddy	No	Plugins	Plugins

The difference between WordPress.com and WordPress.org is that WordPress.com will host your website, which means all you do is sign up and get started creating site content; on the other hand, WordPress.org is open source software, which means you download and install it on your own web server. Of the people interested in WordPress, probably most would be well served by WordPress.com, which simply requires setting up a free account to start with and graduating to a paid account when traffic picks up. While setting up your own site seems to give you more control, in fact, managing your own site is a time-consuming process which can also open you up to security challenges and site maintenance problems. You have a business to set-up and operate and you don't want to be setting up and hosting your website yourself. In addition, if you don't secure your site properly, you will face everything from random defacement to serious security holes. Just as you would not set up a generator to power your business, but instead would sign up for electricity service and pay per use for the utility, the smartest way to set up a site is to use a hosted service. Of course, you must select a reliable webhost to do the job for you and focus on developing meaningful content that can communicate what you do. Many would likely opt for a paid account which allows for a custom domain name and added space. This option gives you the software that has a huge selection of templates to choose from so that you can find the right look and feel, a large user community, lots of how-to books, and plenty of web information to give you tips and tricks that are all slightly easier to use than WordPress.org.

We will be more adventurous for the book (partly because we are geeks who like to re-invent the wheel every now and then) and go with the slightly more complicated WordPress.org software module hosted on our GoDaddy website. This method is still not difficult because GoDaddy, like many web host providers, has a menu option that says, "Install WordPress," and allows you to specify a folder on your web site for the WordPress software. The advantage to this approach is that all of the WordPress files are copied into your folder and can then be modified, allowing for more customization and the ability to include third party plugins. For example, financial eCommerce is supported through plugins. As of September 25, 2013, our GoDaddy account costs $4.49/ month with unlimited websites, bandwidth, disk space, and at no extra charge for WordPress.

An honorable mention goes to FourSquare, which offers simplicity with integration of blog, web support, email list support, and the financial side of ecommerce. To over simplify it a bit, their rates are $8/ month for blogging, $16/ month blogging and email management, and $24/ month for blogging, email, and financial eCommerce. FourSquare excelled at ease of use and for simple integration of its tools. In this world of almost free online tools, it's priced slightly higher than others, but may be worth it for the reduced headaches. It is intended for users who do not want to be web programmers, and it offers flexible editing without all-out site design. If you plan on doing your own logistics for sales, but want simple integrated payment systems, and if an easy integrated site sounds good, FourSquare may be for you.

From our point of view, honorable mention goes to Posthaven for their straight forward and unusual pledge to host your blogs forever. Their clean design was liked best by many of our viewers during the Blog SmackDown. Although the site did not have extensive templates, the basic functional design was appreciated. Since many of the features are not ready, and we need to get blogging this fall (2013), we will still stick with the WordPress direction for the book. Depending on when you read this, you may want to check out their site and see what has become of a neat idea. Tweet us if we should take another look.

Google's Blogger deserves a mention. Started in 1999 and associated with Google since 2002, it remains a reliable choice. The service is free and easy. Possibly a good choice if you have a solid web strategy and want to add a blog.

The runners up were Movable Type and Type Pad. Still solid choices with a track record of good customer service.

How to Use WordPress

Before I started this book, I though WordPress was cool, but after putting some time into investigating its competition and its features, I think it is amazing! Matt Mullenweg is another one of those young guys who quit school, typed (quite) a few lines of (awesome) code, and made a fortune, which, of course, makes the company sound all the more cool. Why did I stay in school! I keep kicking myself.

Anyway, as I mentioned earlier, there are two ways to go with WordPress: the WordPress.com and WordPress.org routes. WordPress.com is set up as a service. You sign up, pay a fee, and the software is hosted on their site, and you just start customizing away. WordPress.org is really a supplier of the software as a free open source product. You just download it and put it in a folder on your web server. In a way, there are really two ways to go with this as well. You can literally download it and place it in a folder then do a couple configuration things to get it to talk to the database; however, many of the web service providers will have a button or a menu option that say something like "Install WordPress." So the approach that we took for the book was to get a web hosting account at GoDaddy and push the install WordPress button. We put it in the root folder of the web server because we are doing the whole webpage as well as blogging with WordPress. We could have put it in a subfolder if we wanted to do something different for the home page and then just use WordPress for blogging. Decisions, decisions, but I think you get the picture. What we say here, though, applies to using WordPress in any of those combinations, unless we mention otherwise.

As we mentioned earlier, a blog is really just a set of postings stored to a database rather than just written on the webpage. The advantage of this is that a program can query the databases and display them any which way, such as by author, by posting time, by the one with most comments, or the least, or even backwards. And web pages that work with databases are becoming easier and easier to write with the new tools becoming available. This is the reason the custom blog is becoming more popular. Anyway, who wants to write all that database code when we could put that time to good use by blogging about our own expertise? So the point is that WordPress has come up with a pretty good database design with all fields for tracking posting, comments, categories, users, and all the other stuff that just about everyone who is going to blog will need. We just want to give it a look and feel, and organization, and maybe select particular features that will make it work best for us. That is where the WordPress themes come in and why they can be changed. All WordPress sites have the same basic database design (although custom extensions are possible) and include a wide variety of themes to organize and view the data. The posts and the comments are the data, and themes are the lenses to view them through.

So pick a theme and get started! The more the theme has that you want, the less you will have to modify it. Does a theme have what you want? To find the answer to this question will take a little planning on your part. There is the interesting balance between trying to make a plan and going in that plan's direction, and not making a plan and waiting to see where the adventure will take you. Are you ready to cut the dock lines or not? You won't know until you cut them, but by then, it will be too late. So, ideally, you'd like to know what colors you want, how many blogs you want, whether you want web pages without blogging and such. If you have some experience with this, you can make a detailed list. If you don't, try to jot down a few ideas and then give it a try. Don't rush. Search through the available themes, see what features they have, and start narrowing it down. If you are new to this, think of your first project as practice and plan to throw it away. If you cut the dock lines when you are not ready on the web, you just lose a little data, so don't worry.

To get the book blog started, we picked the theme, Parabola. We cut the dock lines on this quickly because we wanted to blog, but the book really is not about blogging, per se, so we wanted to get on with it. When the book is done, I'd like to do version 2.0, but for now, let's see what happens. Most themes have a header section, a footer section, a place to put the blog, and some widgets that can make various directories of the blogs, such as by newest or by category. Parabola had a tool to select color themes, which was cool. Changing each color manually can be tedious, but if you know what you want, that can be fine. We picked a set of colors we liked. Parabola also had multiple menu options including a main menu, a header menu, and a footer menu. I knew I wanted to link to standard stuff, like the Dockside home page and my own, so I liked the different headers. I also envisioned someday getting more books out there, so I liked the flexibility in navigation. Ha. More books might be really getting ahead of myself, but why not dream? Thirdly, it was really easier set up the social networking links, and we all gotta have those.

WARNING: As soon as I cut the dock lines on the blog page, I was inundated with spam, which was mostly random characters and words. In the administrator panel, I think for all themes, under settings/discussion, there is a check box that says, "Users must be registered and logged in to comment." *The default was unchecked. Check it right away.*

So now you have posted some of your wisdom, and you want to know how many bazillion followers have read it. Get the stats. On August 20, 2013, WordPress merged some of its most popular stat plugins and some other helpful plugins into their JetPack plugin. At this point, it seems like everybody needs a JetPack plugin. It will require a login ID on WordPress.com, but there is no cost. Loading JetPack actually loads thirty or so different plugins, many of them needing their own activation, but this makes a good set of plugins to give you a base set of what would have been advanced functions just a couple years ago. First we activated WordPress.com Stats.

A next step is to think about search engine optimization (SEO). You want the search engines to see you, don't you? Well those search engines have different ways to decide how closely a website matches the search terms the person types in. For example, if the keyword is in the title of the site, it is more important than if it is in the main text. So you want the right words in the right place to make the search engine think you are important. Using a search engine plugin allows you to edit those words without going into the html files created by the theme. We looked at a few, not as a serious study, but by then we were getting down to details, so we didn't want to slow down. Yoast seemed pretty good, and the author, Joost de Valk, has a nice article on his site about how to do SEO in general, as well as how to use the Yoast plugin[45].

Joost's first suggestion is to look at the permalink's setting, which is in all WordPress sites[46]. This setting sets the format for creating URL's as they are posted. The default format makes the URL for a post and includes a post number rather than words, so it is not adding much to your search engines priority. Change it to one that includes your article and category name.

Email and Email Lists

Email is the technology that lets you send a digital letter to someone in the Internet. Email is useful in itself to keep up with individual correspondences who might have questions about your business. It can also be used with lists of recipients to broadcast your ideas and update your base of interested followers.

Tim Grahl[47] comments that email is one of the most effective of the social media technologies because the messages end up in your inbox, and as a recipient, you are likely to process each one to some extent, whereas other social network technologies make it easier to skip past much of the content.

To develop an email list, you will have to find people willing to sign up. You can begin with friends and business associates, but you will eventually build to people you do not know. Once people begin discovering your web site, you would like to capture their email address, but you need a way to convince them to give it to you. Tim Grahl suggested being "specific and compelling" in your description of why you are asking for someone's email address. How will it benefit the person signing up and what will they receive. Contrary to its obituaries, email is not dead (like Mark Twain in May 1897), and reports of its death are exaggerations[48].

Email management systems are used to let your fans sign up for your newsletter or some other custom communication. There are two major steps here. Step one is to gather a mailing list with your fans, and step two, the more important step, is to organize that list into categories. Here is the problem with merely amassing a list. You can even buy a mailing list from a list vendor. It is worthless. Most people receive so much spam that they ignore much of the mail sent to the list. Rather, a well curated list of truly interested fans, organized by preferences, is a valuable asset. An opt-in approach, where you get approval from the recipient *before* adding them to your list, is a good idea.

In one case that we saw in our work, a realtor collected email addresses from clients and visitors to open houses. Great idea, back at the turn of the millennium. However, the list proved useless in generating new business. What happened? A quick review showed that most of the people in the list were swamped with e-mail promotions and deleted email from the realtor. What makes sense, in this case, is to find out the interests of the open house visitor. Do they want a bigger house, a smaller one, a more modern design, or a house in another neighborhood, etc? When this goes into the database, the promotion emails are sent to targeted individuals. This makes the list more valuable. As a potential buyer or seller, you are more likely to open an email from a realtor that comes in occasionally rather than one that comes in each week, and if that e-mail is targeted to your interests, it has a high rate of follow-up action, which makes the program valuable.

The guidelines are simple. Sign up potential customers/fans, collect interest information (and allow them to fine-tune it over time), and target the email carefully. Make sure you follow the law regarding spam.

CAN-SPAM laws have rules about who you can include on your email list. If the person has not subscribed through explicit request or other business relationship, you are limited in what you can send. Further, your email must have a place for the recipient to opt out of the list, and you need to comply with their wishes. In addition, your subject line must not be deceptive. You can't send out a mail about an open house with a header that says "Tax Refund." Also, of course, you cannot hide behind spoofed sender addresses. Finally, it is good practice to not include the list of addresses in the email. If you are sending out an e-mail to 50 people, don't just make a list of the 50 addresses, stick in the send to list, and hit Send. The problem, in addition to releasing the list to the entire group, is the Reply All option. Reply All crisis management should be part of the training program for today's networked office.

A good email management system should handle these chores, ensure compliance with the law, and give you a management dashboard to monitor the performance of your email strategy. A good email management system will tell you who opened your letters and how many forwarded them. It will also tell you when the mail was opened, figure who had the most interest, and what topics seemed to be the most appealing.

Ok, ok. Enough of these long winded comparisons of every option. We need to get to the platform for the book operation before the St. Petersburg Power and Sailboat Show so it will be ready for publicity! Actually, the more of it that is ready before the October, 25, 2013 research trip to Marathon, the better. On that trip, we plan to do some research around the town in Marathon, in addition to Dockside, and we really want as much of the platform in place as soon as possible so we can point people toward it as we meet them around town.

Thus we dove right into MailChimp. Eric and Kim use it. Kim has been using it for several years, and it is free to get started. We did a quick Internet search and found some people that gave good reasons for it to be better than Constant Contact. I used Constant Contact about five years ago to get the word out about a research center, and it worked pretty well. However, the reasoning for MailChmp sounded good, so I signed up. MailChimp was founded by Ben Chestnut in 2001[49]. Other email marketing systems are Benchmark Email and Campaigner, but there are many sites in this category.

To allow fans to sign up for your mailing list, you need to give them a place to fill out their information. MailChimp can generate the code that you can cut and paste onto your web page so that fans can add there. It can also give you code for WordPress and generate a tab on your FaceBook page. The Facebook integration was nice and easy. Just let MailChimp log into your account, and you can associate your MailChimp email list with any Facebook page you manage. Afterwards, the Facebook page will have a simple tab at the top, labeled as you wish, that brings up a form for the person to sign up for your mail list.

Once you get some fans, writing to them with a drag and drop editor, which has templates so you can get snazzy forms easily, is simple.

Facebook

Facebook revolves around user accounts and pages that support other concepts such as businesses or brands. Facebook has distinguished itself by being a social media site where users who typically know one another in the real world sustain the connection in the virtual world. Individuals set up accounts for their personal timeline. Sometimes described as a microblog, Facebook is a little like a blog in that you share posting; however, posts are usually much shorter and shared with a group rather than being aimed at the public.

The now famous Facebook was started by Mark Zuckerberg, Eduardo Saverin, Andrew McCollum, Dustin Moskovitz, and Chris Hughes on February 4, 2004. Originally used to share study material and meet other students at Harvard University, it first expanded to other universities and eventually to the general public. Yes, this is another story of college kids cobbling together software in their dorm rooms, gaining some initial traction, quitting school, and making billions. I'm not sure why there are so many of these stories in the software industry, but good for them.

Today, the advantage of the system for those promoting their art or business is that the people are largely being themselves and are communicating with real friends, unlike some chat systems that seem to devolve into anonymous people flaming their aggravations. A high percentage of users signed up for Facebook use their correct identity and are intending communication with people they know in real life.

Facebook originally offered just a mutual friendship relationship, meaning that if one is a friend of another, the relationship is reciprocal and equal. That means in order for your status updates to be read, you would have to have friends and you would also receive their status updates. This symmetric sharing relationship tends to lead to more real friend relationships than a star / fan relationship, which can be more of a broadcast wherein the fan is listening to the updates of the star. Facebook focused on the symmetric relationship for many years, resulting in strong relationships developed between real people.

Since its inception, the following relationship has been added which allows someone to follow the status updates of another without being friends. This method is now commonly used by stars and companies alike to broadcast updates to their fan base. Although it is commonplace for major stars to have large followings, the effectiveness of the following is probably, in part, from Facebook's tradition of having a symmetric relationship with real people. That tradition means that most people are receiving updates from real people, with updates from the stars they follow mixed in, keeping them interested in reading the feed.

Originally, a Facebook account represented the information the user wanted to make known to their friends. With the original design being intended only to share with friends, security was simplistic. Much later, when people began to "friend" people who were only acquaintances, multiple levels of sharing were introduced. Today, for each piece of information a person enters, they can specify whether it is seen by the public, friends, family, friends of friends, or specifically targeted friends. It is also possible to block information to particular friends. Since this level of control of information is applied to each piece of data, the system allows the user a very fine-tuned approach to information sharing. To a certain extent, this may be considered a double-edged sword because the user could mistakenly share the wrong information with the wrong person.

The methods of a business comprised of artists who are keeping in touch with their fans seems to work best when the basis for an ongoing discussion can be found. Touring musicians usually find this easy because there are many stories from the road that can be shared. Fans can share requests for future events, such as potential tour stops or types of recordings. When a musician can fulfill the requests, there is a good opportunity to take the distance out of the relationship between fans and artists that could exist when just traditional media is used. Companies like Ford, for example, also use Facebook, and they constantly look for ways to engage fans in a conversation. For example, I like the posts of "The Coolest Mustangs of All Time" posted by the owners of the Mustang Facebook page.

Of course, you no longer get only what you want to get in your Facebook feed. Page owners can pay a fee to have their page featured in front of Facebook users who are not followers or friends. Facebook places the likes to the page in the news feed of users who might have a related interest or fit a similar demographic. Note, however, the click trough rate on those unrequested items is much smaller than those on posts seen by people who requested to be friends or followers.

Twitter

Twitter is a group messaging site that uses short messages, which are sometimes called microblogging. Originally limited to plain text messages with a maximum length of 140 characters, Twitter now allows links to photos and videos. The messages are still the 140 text characters, but the photo is uploaded to Twitter and given a short URL. The cute little messages are called "tweets." Tweets provide sufficient length to communicate an idea, but force the user to condense it to fit the limit of the medium. Why have tweets worked so well? The answer may lie in the origin of the 140 character message length. According to Friedhelm Hillebrand, a German telecommunications engineer who designed the short messaging service standardly used in the GSM cellular system, this is not an arbitrary value, but, rather, is based on the length of many typewritten statements. Yes, back in 1985, when the standard was developed, people used typewriters! The original length was 160 characters, with 20 used for addressing. SMS rides on the control channel used by cell towers to manage their operations, and hence, is typically more reliable than voice calls, which use more bandwidth and are managed by the control system. Incidentally, in the

U.S., texting surpassed calling in 2007, one year after Twitter made its debut.

In Twitter, the "follow" relationship is asymmetrical in that users can choose who they want to follow without the other user necessarily following them. It works well in the performer-fan model. Eric could easily keep fans updated while on tour. Followers can reply to the person whom they are following specifically, but when that person posts original tweets, these tweets only go to followers. If you follow a great band like Eric's, and your friends follow you, you can easily retweet the tweets you receive from Eric so that your friends will see them.

Twitter was launched by Evan Williams (remember Evan Willams from Blogger above), Noah Glass, Jack Dorsey, and Biz Stone, among others who influenced it, in March 2006. Remember, Williams made his millions from selling Blogger to Google, and had bought a nice house and car, and started a new company called Odeo. Odeo was intended to get into the Podcasting business, but with Apple adding it to iTunes, that model looked dead. However, some of the Odeo techs brainstormed what would become Twitter. By July 2012, Twitter had passed 1 billion users. While still about half as many users as Facebook, this amount was enough to make it the second biggest social networking site (Lunden, 2012). On November 7, 2013, Twitter went public with a market capitalization of around $23B (give or take a billion since it was still fluctuating). The story of Jack, Evan, Noah, and Biz is really well-told in the book, *Hatching Twitter*, by Nick Bilton (2013), which I recommend as a read for those who like to learn about the people behind tech start-ups. Nick clearly makes you feel the gut-wrenching moments, like when Evan was going to puke before he made his last speech to the Twitter staff before being kicked out, or when Jack and Noah had a drunken exchange about what this whole status genre was doing. Geeze, this is sounding like a book review. OK, I liked it.

Eric and Kim do more Facebooking than tweeting, as I do myself, so I thought it would be good to talk with someone who tweets first. I had the pleasure of having coffee with a Twitter confidant of mine, Lindsey

83

Hamlin, on a cold November day in New Orleans. OK. New Orleans is not that bad compared to some other places, but the wind was blowing around 25mph. She really helped me get focused on thinking of Twitter as a set of conversations and looking at joining them based on your interests. For the past few months, I had spent a lot more time in Facebook than Twitter. We both agreed that more of the Twitter conversations seem to follow professional interests rather than friend relationships, like in Facebook, so this may be a good place to connect with others who are interested in crowdfunding. My previous experience with Twitter had been more in the followers-listening-to-experts' mode, which works too. I like following Yoast tweets because I use their SEO plugin for WordPress, and sometimes I get an idea I can run with. However, conversations give you a two way street: one, to learn more about your field from the leading names, and two, to comment on where your niche may be or on a new direction you are developing in the field.

If you have found someone interesting to follow, check out who they follow. Lindsey suggested I follow Karim R. Lakhani, @klakhani, because of my interest in crowdsourcing. He claims to be an expert social janitor. Hmm. . . I'll have to figure out what that is, but sounds related to crowdsourcing. As of this writing, he is following 1,129. Let's see who looks interesting among them. There are a couple links to the Nest thermostat people. I love their thermostat, but that's not what I'm looking for now. Many of his followers have no description. (Note to self: fill out the "about me" blurb in Twitter in case anyone is reading about you in a list of followers or following [followingers?]). I found he was following a number of people that captured different things I might be interested in, but on that day, I wanted to stay on target with crowdfunding, or at least related social networking. I found Pinar Yildirim (@Pinar_Wharton) who is a Marketing professor at Wharton who studies "New Media, Advertising, Networks, Online Platforms." I'll follow her. Chris Sacca @sacca invests in Twitter and Kickstarter. Off the subject, but I will follow him in case we crowdfund the printing of Dockside. Mike Morris, @mpmorris36, says he is using the crowd to move people to the Cloud. Can't pass that up. Anyway, you get the idea, but it will take a little snooping. I'll probably look for who Pinar likes next.

Lindsey also discussed the art of composing your tweet. Of course, you only have the 140 characters, but you need to fit your hashtag and URL in there, as well as include an engaging comment. Bitly is a URL shortening service that can reduce the size of the URL you want to share with people and leave you with more room for your message. Bitly is good because you can use it with any service. Twitter has updated to its own service that adjusts all-included URLs. If you put the bitly URL in Twitter, it still comes out as the Twitter twenty-two character standard.

As a comparison, though, I put http://tropnetworking.com/ in bitly and it shortened it to http://bit.ly/1a5eap2, twenty-six characters to twenty-one, or a 19.2% reduction. Of course, if you put in a perma link to a blog page, you get a better reduction ratio. When I put in the link to my blog post on burger tasting at Dockside (http://tropnetworking.com/dockside-book/2013/11/03/burgers-beach-bob-coldies/)

I got http://bit.ly/17uEt9q. Seventy-seven characters to twenty-one, or a 72.7% reduction. So I decided to give Google URL shortner a fair try. They reduced my site to http://goo.gl/7RDz8P. Twenty characters, one character better, or a 74.0% reduction from the original.

Instagram

Instagram was founded by Kevin Systrom and Mike Krieger[50]. Both Stanford grads who had worked in the tech industry, including a stint at Twitter for Kevin, they saw a need for a social site with a focus on pictures.

Video support was added in June 2013[51]. Today, the site is still heavily used for pictures and videos and is well known for the easy special effects that can be applied to the pictures and videos just before uploading. Posts include a photo or video, text comments, hash tags, and at signs. Readers can comment, like, and share posts. Asymmetrical following is allowed to receive other users' posts in your news feed. The photos and videos format to a square aspect ratio, which give the retro appearance of old polaroids, but does not support the newer standards in wide formats.

As of October 1, 2013, the app was available from Instagram for iOS and Android. Also available was 6tag for Windows phones, which was developed separately by Rudy Huyn. Rudy set up 6tag so that it could post to the 6tag servers and then send the posts, fairly seamlessly, to Instagram through the Instagram API. While Instagram posts can be shared with other social services, like Twitter and Facebook, support for other networks is being developed.

Instagram is planning on adding ads in 2014[52].

Graphic and Photo Editing

Even if you are not a graphics artists, you will eventually probably want to design a logo or retouch a photo for posting to the web or one of the other social networking sites. We chose Corel Paintshop Pro because it was full featured and on sale. We also chose Corel VideoStudio Pro X6 for video editing.

Aspect Ratio

Aspect ratio is the ratio of the height to the width of a picture or video. Aspect is good to keep in mind because it affects how well you might be using your screen space or the compatibility of a photo or video with an online tool. HDTV now has a standardized aspect ratio of 16:9, meaning a picture 16 inches wide would be 9 in inches high. We use this as good place to start a picture or video, unless there is a reason do something different. 16:9 is also the default format for DVD's. The film industry often uses 1.85:1 and 2.39:1, which are wider formats that result in black matting at the top and bottom when displayed on an HD TV. Old time TV's and computers were usually 4:3 (much closer to square). New computers are usually 16:9 or similar. A nice discussion of aspect ratio can be found at Wikipedia.[53]

Colors

The web allows for more than 16 million colors. You will want the colors you choose in your logo to match those you use in your web page, so it helps to know a little about web colors. Technically, a web color is defined by a six digit hexadecimal, or base 16, number such as 00FF00 (which I chose for the green in Trop Networking [tropnetworking.com]). The most common colors also have a standard word associated with them; for example, 00FF00 is also called green. The numbers are needed, though, if you choose shades that do not have the standard words. Further, some colors go better with other colors, so you may end up picking three complimentary colors for your web site design. I'm not an artist and cannot pick colors, but a nice site with recommendations for picking complimentary colors is Color Scheme Designer at: (http://colorschemedesigner.com/).

Picture File Formats

Use GIF for small logos and jpeg for photos. When using a graphics editors, such as Corel Paintshop Pro, store files in the native format of the software (in this case pspimage) until the work is complete and then save in the file format for the target environment.

Video Editing

Video creation, editing, and publishing has become quite easy with modern technology; however, the amount of skill and time required to make a professional looking production, and one that looks homemade, is still considerable. You might divide the process into three steps: video capture, editing, and publishing. In this section, we note a few of the approaches than can be used at a low cost.

Capturing video can be done with equipment ranging from a smart phone to a high-end studio camera that costs thousands of dollars. The smart phone does pretty good. The handheld camcorder still has a place in that it has an analog zoom which allows you to zoom without degrading resolution. For example, if a camera has a fixed lens and uses digital zoom, it is really just blowing up the pixels it has already collected to make a part of the picture the size of the whole. That works to some extent, but eventually, the result is too low a resolution to be clear. Sound capture is an integral part of video capture and can be done with microphones built into the camera of external microphones. The built in microphone on a camera has a limited range, and is able to pick up background sounds so that it can work in a quiet close-up setting. For longer distances, a microphone may be needed to be placed by the subject. A wired microphone can be used, but inexpensive bluetooth microphones are emerging to make wireless fairly inexpensive and easy.

Editing involves putting together the captured pieces of video, carving them down to size, and adding effects. Your video may have segments that were captured at different times, such as the interviews shown in Eric's crowdfund video. These segments can be combined using video editing software. Each segment can be edited to just include the best or most relevant part. After the segments have been put together, effects, such as titles at the beginning and end of the video, transitions between segments, and background music, can all be added. Although the software is generally easy to use, one should not underestimate the time needed to tweak some of these details. There are many pieces of software on the market for both Microsoft Windows and Macintosh platforms. Eric used Final Cut Pro on the mac to edit his crowdfund video. I have been using Corel Video Studio while my technical editor has been using Camtasia.

When the editing has been completed, the software renders it into a single file in a particular video format at a particular resolution. For example, the MP4 video format is quite common. The video can be published to the web by uploading it to the account where you have your web page; however, to make the video work for all viewers, you should have multiple formats and resolutions because readers will vary in what browser or device they are using. Uploading to YouTube solves this problem because YouTube makes multiple file formats from the one you upload by using its own software to detect what type of browser a viewer is using so that the viewer sees the correct format. Once uploaded, you can still place a view of the video in your web page with the embed HTML that YouTube provides. The embed HTML are particular HTML codes that you can copy and paste from YouTube into your web page, so the video shows in your page as if it were stored on your web site, keeping you from having to go through the hassle of figuring out the formats.

For this sequential process, from capture to publishing to work, some amount of planning is needed. For example, deciding what segments will be at what locations and with which people will help with scheduling the capturing of all the segments needed. Further, deciding that a segment is not right while you're editing may delay the process as you find a way to reshoot the segment. However, keep in mind, particularly if you are new to this, it is a learning process. By the time you have captured, edited, and produced a video, you will have learned how to do it better. Try to leave time and patience to redo what you have done. Your second iteration will look surprisingly more polished.

Financial Transaction Systems

PayPal has become the premiere financial transaction processing system of the web. Fundable uses WePay.com. The financial transaction processing system allows your customer to use the standard range of credit and debit cards for their payments and send the payments to your account.

PayPal uses a proprietary risk management algorithm to detect for fraudulent vendors that may be trying to collect funds as part of a scam.

The risk management algorithm has proven a problem for crowdfunding as well as other entrepreneurs who may experience fast increases in business in the early stages of their enterprise while not having a long track record.

Alexa

Alexa is a web site analytics company that monitors Internet traffic to develop metrics on web site usage. The site offers a number of free metrics as well as paid monitoring services. Founded in 1996, it focuses on multiple measures of global web traffic to determine the usage of a web site[54]. The site offers free data about the top 100,000 sites in the world and can be used as a rough measure of the site popularity. As of this writing, tropnetworking.com has not made the top 100,000, but I am hopeful.

Podcasting

On March 17, 2013, Eric launched *Eric Stone Radio*, a radio show he could tailor for his fans. The show uses Podcasting technology which allows the podcaster to develop audio content that is delivered to the subscribing audience. The podcaster can post new content at pretty much any interval, and the subscriber can listen at his or her convenience, so it is more like an on-demand radio than the traditional format. Eric's launch date of March 17 put him in a good position to add more content and support for Dockside and the Dockside Fundable campaign. As mentioned earlier, his July 14, 2013, episode gave an update on the Fundable campaign.

Eric uses the email address, askeric@ericstoneradio, as a way to collect questions from fans. He also answers questions that come in through other tools, such as Facebook.

Orchestrating the Tools

With all of these tools available, you have to decide which tools to use at what time in order to convey what information. One way of thinking about it is to consider the length of the content and whether it is just a sentence or several paragraphs, and how the length of time that the content will be relevant. For example, a web page tends to have longer detailed content that is relevant for some time, maybe months or years, whereas a Twitter tweet is a short message that may only be relevant for the moment. Although these are not hard rules, the general relationship between the tools is shown in Figure 8.

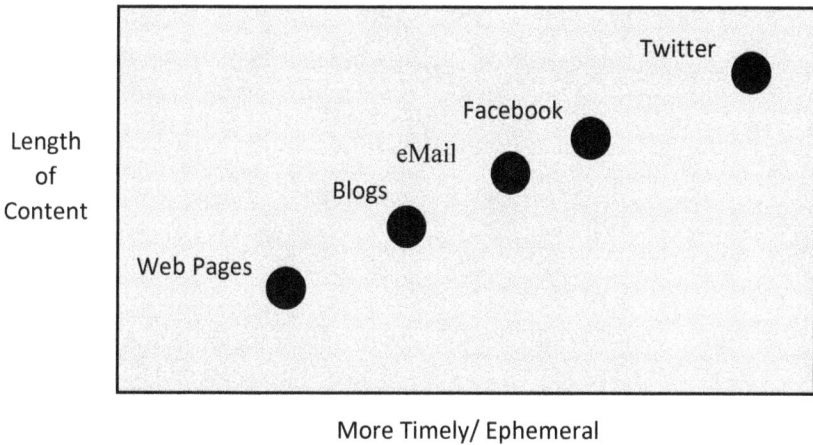

Figure 8: *Relative Dynamics of Social Networking Tools*

However, this is a simplified view. Although email is shown in the middle as being medium in length and having a medium amount a time relevance, it is the most powerful category when you would like your fans to take action. Because it shows up in your fans' email inbox with other relevant correspondences, it takes on more importance than the other tools. It is also a tool that should not be overused; for the same reason, fans may become annoyed and opt out of future correspondence.

The web page tends to be the anchor for the platform. When a fan wants to proactively look for the status of your project, that is the first place they will look. It should be kept up-to-date with basic contact information as well as more long term information, such as business hours or the menus for a restaurant.

By contrast, Facebook page updates are relevant just over the next days or hours. A reminder of tonight or tomorrow's event would be appropriate as well has the announcement of an award or a new milestone.

Chapter 4: Marathon, FL

Now that the crowdfund had been completed and the Dockside renovations were well underway, I wanted to venture back to Marathon to see how things were progressing. Leaving from my home in Baton Rouge by way of US Interstate 10 had me reflecting on the diversity of the places you can visit on I-10. I-10 shoots across the lower part of the United States from Jacksonville, Florida, to Santa Monica, California, crossing great swaths of Americana from the not-so-south of Florida, across the really-south of Alabama and Louisiana, on to Texas and then to the Southwest desert states, and then on to the glitter and grunge of Santa Monica before hitting the Pacific Ocean. The desert area of Tucson must be the most beautiful place in the country with its flowering saguaro and its soaring mountain tops around the hot and low valley of downtown. Coyote still chase road runner there. West Texas is a desert without the flowers, but hey, it has oil. I lived in Midland for a while, between boom cycles in the oil industry. We had one bar in town called The Bar, where a big Texas rib eye, a cold Bud, and pretty hopping band got you through the night. I wish I was there during the booms, though. Sounds fun. Timing is everything.

That morning, I was using I-10 for the important little jaunt from Baton Rouge to the Louis Armstrong International Airport in Kenner, outside New Orleans, to pick up the short Southwest flight to Key West. I estimate that I have driven this little section more than 3000 times, but, filled with anticipation for Marathon, this drive would become one of the more memorable.

Heading East from Baton Rouge in the morning, you miss the congestion of the commuter traffic heading the other way and speed out into swamp country. Only one Starbucks all the way to New Orleans, so better get a dark roast while you can. Sipping on that for about forty-five minutes with Pandora blaring Trop Rock, you hit the most amazing rise in the highway. First you see the bright sunrise and then the vast expanse of Lake Pontchartrain. Look across the water, and the skyscrapers of downtown New Orleans gleam like a mini-city island. Once you cross the Bonne Carre spillway, you have crossed over from the mainland to a different kind of place that I like to think of as the island after Key West.

It was really cool to have direct flights on Southwest from New Orleans to Key West. It is a quick hour and twenty minute hop from one kind of paradise to another, and at not too bad a price. This trip can now happen more often. Southwest is off the B terminal and boasts a Zatarains as the main restaurant and a bar past the security. They have a pretty nice breakfast with dirty rice and biscuits. Unfortunately, when I got there, they were all out of Bloody Mary mix. How could that be? Sometimes paradise runs out. Sadly, Southwest has discontinued this service, putting New Orleans and Key West a little bit farther apart.

On Southwest, you don't have the typical assigned seating of other airlines, so, according to your boarding number, you line up next to your assigned pole just outside the gate. Some people rush to be at the front of this line so that they can have a good pick of seats, but if you do this and you are flying alone, be aware that while you can pick your seat, you cannot pick your seat neighbor. Your seat neighbor will eventually pick you! My number was forty-five and was located about a little more than halfway back on the plane. I picked a cute blond sitting by herself to be my neighbor for the next hour and a half. It turns out, I made a good pick. Leona was from New Orleans and was also a fan of Eric

Stone's. I guess his fans are everywhere. She was retired and going to get some R & R time in Key West on her brother Captain Bob's boat. She gave me the meet-up information for that night's local parade. Apparently, I had arrived on the Friday of Fantasy Fest. No wonder Eric and Kim were driving the Sprinter out to meet me in Key West. Fantasy Fest is sort of Mardi Gras meets Halloween in Key West, and is held in late October. There are parades with food and drink served on the main streets. If you are travelling to Marathon by way of Key West and get distracted, it can end up taking an extra day to get to Marathon. Adventurers need to keep an eye open for opportunity.

Once in Key West, I parked my rental car on the side street next to Hemmingway's house because I thought I should check in on this great writer and adventurer whose path I may someday follow. Well, some parts of his path. I probably won't do the boxing thing and, hopefully, another world war won't break out. You can still see his second floor study where he used to write. A small table in the middle with a manual typewriter. I was in awe of the volume of his work when I saw the typewriter it was written on. It was not made by Microsoft! After Hemingway's, it was time to be opportunistic and grab a coldie at the Green Parrot while waiting for Eric and Kim. After we met up, we checked out the Key West parade scene and then headed to Marathon, about an hour away, along that magical stretch of Highway 1. The milemarker 0 for Highway 1 is in Key West, and the city of Marathon is from about milemarker 47 to 60.

Marathon, FL, often called the heart of the keys, is located about midway between the mainland and Key West, and is home to its own charm, with interesting shops, restaurants, and island fun spots featuring great Trop Rock music, among other things. It has long been a supply center and a coastal connection for sea traders and pirates alike. The name Marathon was established in about 1908 with the naming of the railroad station[55]. The establishment of the railroad began the first lasting population boom with barracks being built for railroad workers and other supporting services, such as the post office, being quickly erected to hasten the completion of the railroad. Building the area had become a marathon. Of course, the hidden harbors of Vaca Key, the largest of the islands making up Marathon, had long been used by European traders and Native Americans alike for provision, although no established community had taken hold for an extended period of time. Today, it remains a great provisioning destination for near-shore boaters as well as Caribbean commuters. The amount of inlets and mangroves make for serene kayaking with clear views down into the marine life and lush green foliage above the water line.

Not long after getting back to Marathon, I went over to Dockside to see how the reservation was going and to see what Eric was working on.

"Ken, do you like painting?" Eric said enthusiastically.

"Sure, sounds fun," I said, but I was thinking I came in my good flip-flops and really didn't want to get paint on them.

After some work on the bar, Eric said, "Now we have to go to Lowe's in Homestead to get 6 inch pvc. Ken, are you ready for a road trip?"

"Sure, I can type notes on the way."

Homestead. What a drag, but I guess you got to hit the mainland every once in a while for supplies. Google put the trip at 1 hour 39 minutes each way. Heck. That was longer than my flight from New Orleans to Key West! Luckily, my laptop battery could go about that long, and I could keep typing. Kind of like Hemmingway writing from a Jeep during the war. Well, not really, but man, you have to admire his tenacity (um, if you are not one of his ex-wives, that is, but they mostly got book royalties, so that's not too bad either).

Eric took the iPhone from his ear and updated us. "Just priced out how much it will cost to install the glycol beer chiller. They cost a small fortune, but they are worth it. The beer chiller takes the beer down to 33 degrees. And we'll have 12, not 10, taps running through it."

"Wait, I thought beer could go colder?" I prodded for more details for the book.

"Beer freezes around 28, so you can only go down to about 33 at the tap. Now the glass chiller will go down to 23 degrees."

All I was thinking was that a 33 degree beer in a 23 degree glass would be perfect, but it would slow my writing, so I would have to put that off until later.

Later, we stained the bar-top with ipswitch pine, but everybody agreed it was too light and would have to be done in a darker stain. It turned out too light the second time and had to be redone again. However, the hard work and experimentation was well worth it once we saw the final result, a rich dark color, and the embedded logos. Eric did a good job of applying his artistry to any of the side jobs that came along with opening his own business.

After the staining, we cleared the debris off the dock for a wine and spirits tasting from one of the distributors. Many of the new staff were there.

The next morning, as often would be the case, Eric woke up with a trip to Home Depot. This time, he was probably going after the mahogany stain.

Turtle Hospital

While there, I took the time to see The Turtle Hospital, which is a couple miles down the A1A from Dockside. The lime green hospital and hotel is dedicated to helping turtles. They are the first "turtle" hospital in the United States, and the only one certified. Originally opened as a hotel in the early eighties, the owners had an interest in marine life and used the largest pool by the sea as a salt water aquarium and stocked it with a variety of fish. Eventually, they started letting the local school kids come and look at the fish. The owners received a lot of questions about turtles and why they didn't have any. They did some research on turtles, learning a lot about the desperate state of the sea turtle world wide, and decided they should devote the facility to the rescue, rehabilitation, and release of sea turtles.

Loggerheads, a threatened species, eats conch. They don't have teeth, but their jaws are powerful enough to crush the conch shells and get to their feast. These turtles used to be killed in large numbers in shrimp nets. The turtles are air breathing, with lungs, so if a fishing net keeps them underwater, they drown. In 1992, a law was past requiring fishing nets to have turtle protectors that kept the turtles out of the net.

Chefs have had to adapt their recipes. A one time, the sea turtle was considered a delicacy in turtle soup and a hot dish of Key West. Today, sea turtles are protected, so turtle soup in the U.S. is made only from fresh water turtles.

The leatherbacks are the largest turtles, getting up to the size of a ton by eating jellyfish. They consume 75% of their weight in jellyfish, their favorite food. They can dive 4,000 feet deep. The pressure would crush a hard shell, but the soft leatherbacks can handle compression. This is the only turtle still in decline. Commercial long-lining kills the leatherback by trapping them under water. They can only hold their breath for about an hour and a half.

The number one threat to our sea species is trash! Plastics look like jelly fish when floating in the water, and the turtles eat it, but they cannot digest it, and it clogs their digestive track and sometimes kills them. The hospital can help them pass their, um, digestion and nurse them back to strength before releasing them.

Turtles living in polluted waters are catching a virus. The hospital can clean the turtle of the virus and the turtle usually becomes immune to the virus and can live on.

Some turtles get hit by boats, squeezing air from their lungs and into the space between the shell. The turtles then become "floaters" and cannot dive for food. The hospital can add weights to the shell to help them dive, but the weights fall off as the turtle grows and its shell molts.

At the back of the hospital are the tanks for the turtles in various stages of rehab. Some will go through rehab and be released while others will remain in permanent residence. The turtles begin with a private room (tank) where their major ailment of injury can be treated. These smaller tanks are filled with different levels of water depending on the turtle's condition. Some are too weak to swim very much, so they need shallow water to allow them to breath without exerting themselves. When strong enough to swim, the water level is raised, and they swim a majority of the time. Sleep for the turtle means taking in a big gulp of air and laying on the bottom of the tank at a reduced energy level so that their air lasts longer. In the wild, they may lean under rocks or coral to keep them from moving or floating with less effort.

And, yes, apparently the turtles have Internet access in their rooms and may keep up with their blogs. Archie, for example, just came in with a lung infection, but it seems like he is progressing. Check out the turtle blogs at: http://www.turtlehospital.org/blog/?page_id=400.

Dolphin Research Center

Not be left out, the dolphins are taken care of on the other end of Marathon at the Dolphin Research Center[56]. Jayne Shannon-Rodriguez and Armando "Mandy" Rodriguez started the place in 1984. The Dolphin Research Center webpage tells of the sites long history with dolphins and other marine life, dating back to the 1940's when Milton Santini used dynamite to create deep gulf lagoons. He seemed to have a pretty independent vision. Today, that center is designed to be a lifetime home for dolphins who cannot be reintroduced to the wild.

Unfortunately, I did not get a chance to visit, but as luck would have it, Charlie Imes was playing at Dockside Tropical Café (after its opening). He told me his story about visiting the Dolphin Research Center, which was so cool that I wanted to retell it here.

Back in 2012, Charlie stopped in to the Dolphin Research Center while on his way to Meeting of the Minds (MotM), an annual meeting of Parrot Heads (the Jimmy Buffet followers). While at the center, he had an introduction to the dolphin experience. Charlie went in carrying his guitar because he did not want to leave it in the hot car. They said since they let him in for free, he should play a song. He played a song, and they asked if he had played it for the dolphins. A little surprised, he said no, he hadn't, and asked why. The staff told him that the dolphins would really react well to that. He was intrigued and said he would stop on his way back from MotM. He and Rick Schettino, another musician, did in fact stop on their way back and played an acoustic set for the dolphins. They took their acoustic guitars out to the dock and started to play. The dolphins slowly came over, two or three at a time, and held their heads out of the water, clearly moved by the music. Charlie recounts the most amazing thing was seeing the dolphins' reaction and seeing it in their eyes. Sometimes, the dolphins would reach up out of the water and do a little dolphin dance or sing with their click to the tune. The musicians didn't need to play particular songs or sing much, just play guitar chords. Rick made a video that can be found in FaceBook (https://www.facebook.com/video.php?v=4508885272983&set=vb.101 6121136&type=2&theater). Charlie has been back since to brighten the day for the dolphins and still is amazed at the experience.

Burgers, Beach, Bob, and Coldies!

By late that sunny Sunday morning, it was approaching a nice 85 degrees outside, and the kitchen staff was back at Eric and Kim's apartment making some experimental "cheeseburger in paradise" recipes. They were going to test some spice mixes, mash a few of the mash-up burger recipes, and cook them all up on the beach for the staff. Hopefully, Eric would bring an acoustic later, but for now, recipes had to be created.

The latest menu that I saw had five carnivorous delights, including one big enough to please Bob Bitchin himself, and four of the Dock's soon to be signature mash-up's. The mash-up concept comes from mashing two different songs together, creating new sounds but with flavors from each. In the case of the burgers, Eric was mixing the flavors into the ground beef. Note that these would be among many other delicacies tested for the Dockside menu, but today would be the day of the burger. I don't know if there will be changes, but this is the latest list of burgers:

- Bob Bitchin's Big Bad Beach Burger
- Mash Up's
  - Bacon Blue
  - South of the Border
  - Hawaiian
  - Greek

At the time, it was still early in the process of crafting the menus that would finally be used at Dockside. It was easy to brainstorm what could become a great long menu, but we had to consider that menu has to be produced in the kitchen and sometimes it is better to trim the menu back to a number of high-quality items that can be delivered in a timely way. For then, though, we could try a variety.

First the staff began working with Eric to get the right spice mix that would be mixed in with the ground beef. Scott and Yolanda were giving their opinions on how much of each spice, salt, pepper, garlic, and others to add to the mash-ups.

The mash-up concept, a la Dockside, is to mix amazing tasty ingredients into the certified Angus ground beef so that delicious flavor comes through in every bite, more so than a traditional "topped" burger. But to add to that flavor, each mash up would be topped with its own custom slaw that would complement the flavor of the burger. Since the bacon-blue recipe was pretty much in the can, today we would focus on the other three.

First up were the Greek burgers, loaded with feta and infused with Greek flavors. The Greek, of course, had its own unique slaw designed to drive the Greek flavor up a notch. The staff pattied these up into trays of eight, each demonstrating their skills at efficiently shaping a burger at the target half pound weight. They also discussed what the real world prep routine might be in order to have fresh burgers shaped without delay to customers.

Next up was the Hawaiian burger, which was to be served with Hawaiian slaw. The cooks were debating about how much ham vs. teriyaki belonged in this one. There were a lot of critical issues still to be worked out on the Hawaiian. For example, should the pineapple be chopped and mashed in, or included in the slaw, or even sliced as a topper. I think Scott suggested staying away from the slice so all the burgers would exemplify the mash up concept. Still that did not rule out pineapple in the slaw. Any combination would be great.

Finally, they prepared the South of the Border mash-up, which was bound to be a favorite for the many beef and cheese fans. The South of the Border would have colby, Jack, and cheddar cheeses along with green chilis. It would be topped with a jalepeno ranch slaw. The staff talked about whether the slaws would work with other dishes, such as fish tacos. They were thinking ahead to some of the kitchen management issues that needed to be worked out to produce quality food in a timely manner, even during a busy dinner rush.

For example, the staff mentioned that if there are four different slaws for all the different burgers, they would need separate containers in the fridge, which might then need to be expanded. Eric wondered if he could add a fridge to the kitchen area, but that was not our focus for that day.

When the prep was finished, the burgers were stacked in layers of wax paper, looking like things of beauty waiting to be grilled.

Kim was tossing up the Goat Salad, commenting, "I could eat goat cheese with everything." The salad included baby greens, red pepper, pecans, cranberries, and, of course, goat cheese. Then it was drizzled with a little extra virgin olive oil. Kim said it was best served with just the olive oil, but anybody should be able to order it with any of the dressings.

As they packed up the goodies, the staff asked about dress code. The staff shirts are tie dyed tee shirts. Someone asked about jeans, and Kim said they planned to avoid jeans. The shirts come in unisex or tank tops.

The beach! Yes, the new burger recipes were then to be brought down to the beach for cooking and tasting. On the way to the beach, we stopped in at Dockside. Two of the newly hired bartenders were painting up a storm. They had painted the speaker doors and the kitchen. They both had plenty of work to keep them busy until opening. I'm not sure they realized how much painting could be involved in bartending, but that's part of the startup process. They both were covered in the paint and sweat of the day, but they had made good progress. The speaker doors would slide into the front of the speaker cabinets to protect the speakers and beautifully decorate the speaker grills when the dock was closed. Eric told them to get cleaned up, pick up some beer, and meet us at the beach! Before we left Dockside, Eric showed me the end of the bar, which he had stained for the third time. This was finally the right color. He was originally going for a light look. From the very light lavender walls to the lightly tanned bamboo, the entire motif was pretty light, but light didn't really work for the bar top. It needed to be a little darker stain to contrast against all the light.

Sombrero beach, just down the end of Sombrero Beach Boulevard, is a great little beach for locals and tourists alike. Probably less than two miles from Dockside, it is one of the nicest beaches in the Keys. With soft white sandy beaches and lined with palms, this makes a great place for a beach party for both kids and adults. Bring charcoal! Charcoal grills, besides pavilions and picnic tables, line the park along the beach. One of the soon-to-be Dockside chefs was put in charge of changing the raw patties into grilled things of beauty. He seared the outside and cooked them to medium. He could tell if they were cooked to medium just by the way they felt when he tapped them on the grill. Each one came out perfect. Eric loaded each with the appropriate slaw and cut them into fourths so that we would all be able to taste each flavor. I think we had about fifteen of the staff and a few fans.

Two longtime fans of Eric's music, Larry and Lisa Everson, had just come in from the cold November weather in Indiana, their home state. They had been facing nights in the 30's and appreciated the change in latitude. They flew into Ft. Lauderdale the day before and stayed a night in Key Largo. They then continued to Marathon to stay the next night. Larry and Lisa talked about how a November visit to the Keys was like putting an extension on summer and a great way to escape before getting back and closing out the work year and completing other responsibilities. As fans of Eric's music, they were excited to see this next phase of Eric's career: starting Dockside. They dove into the burger feast with the rest of us. Larry's favorite was the Hawaiian burger, and Lisa's favorite was the Greek.

The staff made a beautiful cold conch salad that was comprised of yummy onions and tomatoes along with tender conch. Nice! I hoped that got on the menu. Kim brought kettle chips. They were just the packaged ones for the time being. Dockside planned to make homemade kettle chip when they opened. That would be one of the side choices with your gourmet cheeseburger of choice. The next day, I was getting really hungry writing this, and I would need to diet to make up for the previous day's calories.

The first burger to come off the grill was the South of the Border. With cheese, chilies, and jalapeno ranch dressing, the burger grilled up to a creamy flavorful sensation. The chilies were just right, not overpowering, but with a nice zest. You don't have to be a hot and spicy freak to enjoy this one. The concept, a special slaw on the top of each burger, was great. It kept the rich and juicy texture going. After the South of the Border, I had a coldie and jumped in the ocean to cleanse my palate and mind; well, really, there wasn't much going through my mind at that point.

Next off the grill was the Hawaiian. This was a burger, ham, pineapple, and teriyaki sauce burger that came along with its own custom slaw. These burgers probably felt honored at being topped with a slaw made just for them. The Hawaiian burger was still in the experimental stage with different ways of doing the ham. Would it be cut small and mixed in the ground beef, or sliced on top? For that matter, the way to add pineapple was being considered. It could be included in the slaw, included in the ground meat, or sliced and grilled as a topping. In the interest of science, I tried a couple varieties. They were both winners, so I have no doubt the winning recipe will rock.

If pressed, I might have to say the South of the Border was my favorite, but the most surprisingly awesome was the Greek. Man, this was infused with Greekness. Almost tasting like a gyro, but with only beef in it for meat. By the way, how do you pronounce gyro? There seems to be a lot of pronunciations out there, and I can never decide which to use. The infused sauce made every bite taste like a Greek sensation. Here was where the infused ground beefs of Dockside set themselves apart from the places that only vary their burgers by the toppings. This process takes a little more care in the kitchen because they have to prep the five different infused beefs and four different slaws to be cooked up the way you want. I guess it is bar food, but more like gourmet bar food with a gourmet view. Nice!

OK. I almost forgot. The kettle chips that we sampled (not yet the real ones, as I mentioned) were dipped into an amazing fish dip. Dip and chips with your 33 degree draft would work fine, too. I believe the dip will be supplied by an outside supplier rather than being made in-house because it is so good just the way they make it, and they are a local company, so it is still in the Key's family. As of this writing, I won't say who makes it because I don't know if they have made a final decision on that.

As we were all slowing our pace with bellies full of burgers and beer, Eric took out an acoustic and introduced the group to the new house drummer, John. John pulled out a snare drum and some sticks and accompanied Eric on an impromptu, "Rock the Dock," and ear-to-ear smiles were seen around the picnic table. John and Eric had not had much of a chance to practice together, so they just kind of jammed through some of the classics they both new and some of Eric's that John had gotten down from the recordings. All in all, they had a great rapport for just playing together for such a short time. John was able to come in pretty much wherever Eric started up and fill in with some nice impromptu percussions.

Larry and Lisa commented on how awesome it was when Eric pulled out his guitar, noting how it was a different vibe than when watching him on stage. It reminded them of days in Indiana when Eric would play around the fire pit at home. They recalled a time back in Indiana when Eric learned a song in ten minutes from the internet.

This was not your everyday office cook-out thing. There was a beautiful beach scene with gourmet burgers and the cool chance to see Eric relaxed and just having fun while improvising a set with his acoustic. You could see that the staff was really into the vision of Dockside and would bring that afternoon's laid-back party vibe back with them to the Dock.

Later, while we chilled back at the house, Eric and Kim were glad they made it through the day, but it had been a day to remember just like many others had been. We sipped a little rum and hit the hay to get ready for another manic Monday that promised to rise a little earlier than we wanted.

Kim's Got It Covered on Paperwork

On Monday, Eric left the house at about 6 am to hit Homestead. The Lowes trip for PVC kept getting squeezed out by the priorities of the day until it could not be put off any longer.

Assembling the staff to be ready on opening day when there was some uncertainty about the timing presented a challenge. The chicken and egg of hiring employees before there is work, but having them ready when there would be work, was suddenly lots of work.

Kim was totally sick of paperwork. The least fun of paperwork is insurance and taxes. She was also surrounded by to-do lists. She also had to keep up with employee paperwork and licenses. This was also an important time to begin relationships with vendors who hopefully would become long-term partners and build relationships with the staff. She was drafting an employee handbook that would be part of her staff orientation so that everyone, it was hoped, would be working from the same sheet of music.

Harley and Marley, Eric and Kim's two Macaws and company mascots, seemed pretty mellow that morning. Sometimes they were in real need of attention, but they seemed to be comfortable watching the proceedings. During hamburger testing day, they really wanted to help. Harley, knowing how to unlock his cage, came out a couple times. He wasn't sure Eric knew what he was doing with the spices.

Last day to get your info to Kim!

One of the biggest deficiencies with the Fundable site is that it only collected email addresses, names, and credit card information, but not all of the information needed to fulfill an order. So now that the campaign was over, Kim had to send emails to individuals for such information as mailing addresses and shirt sizes. However, since it was almost two months later, not all of the emails were getting responses, and when they did respond, the information was just in text form that had to be retyped.

All, or nearly all, of the fulfillment information needed to be collected so that orders could be produced and shipped. For example, t-shirt sizes were needed so that the right number of t-shirts could be ordered in each size. Depending on how you were having them made, it might not have been cost effective to have them made individually as you received the order information. Further, fans that did submit order information on time would not want to see to much of a delay in fulfillment.

So note to Fundable: add customization to the rewards so that it can be used to gather additional information needed to process rewards.

Software and Systems

They were using Breadcrumb PRO for point of sale (POS). The POS had an iPad interface, so all order changes hit the kitchen or bar in real time. The iPad has an easy interface for changing an order, customizing an order, and even including little extra notes. Quicken is used for payroll and accounting. Quicken prepares information for the accountant. Note that these systems can be tedious. Work to figure out an automated information flow so that this doesn't eat too much time.

At the beach party the day before, I had asked the wait staff what they thought about the iPad system for order taking. They were really enthused and said that having the order transmit to the kitchen in real time was a nice time saver. Actually, I was expecting to see some resistance because I thought a structured system might be a change for the experienced wait staff, but they all agreed it was no problem.

Training, Training, Training!

Eric and Kim needed to attend food manager training. Kim thought it would be an eight hour class. How were they going to fit that in! There must be one person with food manager training on site at all times while the restaurant was open.

Food safety training was required for all servers, and anyone serving alcohol needed to have alcohol safety training. Some of the personnel had been working as servers at other places and already had their certification.

Back to New Orleans

Man, if I can give any advice at all, it is to not go to the Keys for just a weekend. It is way too short a time! You should stay longer, although, probably no matter how long you stay, it won't be long enough.

There is easy rental car return at the Key West International airport. If you drive up early to the airport, just get some extra beach time in across the street. There are great sand views of palms and easy parking so you can hang out and soak up the last rays before crossing the street and returning to the car. If you need a snack, you can drive south a mile to the outskirts of downtown and get a snack and a coldie. Back in the airport, there is a little bar and a sandwich shop. Nothing to write home about, but you'll survive.

An important note about all this is that it was pretty much a day in the lives of Kim and Eric. Most of what I wrote about the restaurant business was observed on a Monday morning while I was drinking coffee. Kim and Eric had been going at that pace for months and would continue to do so into the foreseeable future. So, as of the end of October, the opening appeared to be about two weeks away.

Chapter 5: Developing Your Own Adventure

What adventure do you have planned and how can crowdfunding get you there? It depends on the type of project you have and what your history with your community has been. In Eric's case, he came from a long and successful recording career and made a tack for the blue waters of a restaurant and music venue. Notice the tack made by a sailor, even into new waters, is easier than for a non-sailor. Bob Bitchin's tack towards his new publication, *Cruising Outpost*, while probably personally painful at times, was also the tack of an old seadog. They both could be pretty confident they would not be stuck in irons, a sailing term refereeing to being dead into the wind without enough forward momentum to make a turn.

You may have a long history. We all do, but let's not get into all that here. You need to think seriously about your experience level and notoriety in the field of endeavor, a closely related field, or even in an unrelated field. What is the breadth of your current contacts and their expectations for your project? Although crowdfunding is not a silver bullet, it can be a great way to make the most of organizing your community in a relatively short amount of time. However, the community will be one that is an extension of your other endeavors.

A good example of how the technologies interact and how you can organize your crowd, even without the so called crowdfund technologies, is the launch of Bob Bitchin's second sailing magazine. Bob had been a successful sailing magazine entrepreneur for about seventeen years, years which were built upon many years of publishing a motorcycle magazine and authoring several books. He decided to sell his beloved jewel and retire in the fashion he had become accustomed to, but the deal went south. The magazine was gone, and without the expected pay check. He decided to move on, but his social media technology was all adjusted to sell the old magazine. He had to take that media cannon he had created and recalibrate it for the new magazine, which is about as easy as rolling a cannon from one side of your ship to the other in storm when the enemy takes a turn for the worse.

The first step, then, is to foster community. In this step, you will assess your relationships with your community and look to how they can be improved, leveraging a social platform. The next step will be to discuss crowdfunding with your community so they understand what you are up to and have an opportunity to give you feedback on the direction and implementation. If you feel you are in touch with your community and they have an interest in the project, you can then setup crowdfunding by selecting a crowdfunding provider and developing the social campaign that will be used in the implementation. Once set up, you can pull the trigger and communicate crowdfunding to keep everyone informed that you are live and what progress you are making. Although this can be a hectic phase, the better you have completed the early phase, the better shape you will be in to succeed. Finally, don't overlook the last phase of completing the project. Completing the project entails completing the crowdfund, fulfilling rewards, and possibly most importantly, setting yourself up for what is next. Although the crowdfunding sites describe crowdfunds as a project with a definite beginning and end, your adventure has just begun.

This chapter follows the six step approach that was described in Chapter 1 and shown in Figure 2. The importance of the approach is the recognition that crowdfunding is not an isolated event, but it is embedded in the ongoing adventure.

Foster Community

Who are my Friends?

One of the first early steps in developing a social network technology strategy is to understand what social assets are already in place. When you consider the use of Fundable to raise funds for Dockside Tropical Café, you probably realized that Eric and Kim had a pretty good social following before they began and that following was captured in their email lists, web sites, and Facebook sites. In their case, they leveraged one type of social networking business into another, or maybe just into another phase of the business, depending on how you look at it.

You should assess what social technology assets you currently have in place. If you are thinking of a new venture, does your last line of work have contacts that would be useful? Kim reminds us that the answer to that question is always yes.

On August 8, 2013, we launched the first promotional campaign for the Tropnetworking Facebook page and had a lot fun. I was chatting a mile a minute with Eric's friends and getting a firsthand understanding of how they came to know his music and, in many cases, had become friends with Eric and Kim. It was really more of an inspired launch than a planned launch. Eric and Kim had been driving through Baton Rouge and stopped in for dinner and to check on the progress of the book. I made a big batch of New Orleans style BBQ shrimp, which isn't BBQ at all (but that's really a different story). Pascal's Menale in New Orleans invented it, and it is a wonderful blend of butter, garlic, onion, maybe some Worcestershire sauce for sautéing, and whole head-on shrimp. You serve it in a deep dish, eat the shrimp with your hands, and soak up the sauce with French bread.

Figure 9 shows how the social sites in four of the major social spaces can be used to drive traffic at different points in the crowdfund. Note that for the crowdfund to work, you need to get people to the crowdfund site to participate, but you should first assess where your connections with people are and how those can be developed prior to the crowdfund. Probably, one can argue every social space has some influence on others. In Figure 9, we concentrated on some of the ones we wanted to illustrate to describe how the Dockside crowdfund was driven.

Before Dockside was even a plan, Eric and Kim already had their own individual email lists, Facebook pages, websites, and Twitter sites. They each had LinkedIn pages, both personal and professional. The establishment of these sites already gave Eric and Kim the social network foundation for developing Dockside's social presence.

When planning began for Dockside, Eric and Kim expanded their social presence with a site specific to Dockside. The Dockside web page, Facebook page, and Twitter accounts were set up immediately at the beginning of planning for Dockside, even while the plan was still vague. To establish Dockside's own following prior to the crowdfund, Eric and Kim communicated the evolving plan over the approximately three months from the establishment of the Dockside Facebook page and the Dockside crowdfund. This process was one of converting fans of Eric and Kim from their former work, music and yoga, to the new, more specific project of Dockside. In sailing terms, they signaled the crew they were getting ready to come about. Note that three months should probably be considered a short amount of time to get the word out. Since Kim and Eric's fan base was already tuned into social networks, adding the new sites was not a big change. In your own case, the extent to which you already have a social network in place will signify how much work needs to be done in advance of your launch date.

Eric's close business associate and friend Bob Bitchin was also a player in the social spaces with approximately 20,000 names on his email list. Bob was willing to work with Eric to get the word out ahead of time for the Dockside Facebook page, and then later, during the fund for the Dockside Fundable page. It should be noted that Bob's social spaces are fairly synergistic with Eric's because Bob focuses on the sailing magazines while Eric focuses on the sailing music. The audiences have good overlap in interest, and the number of people who have become friends of Dockside from Bob' announcement is pretty high. Similarly, in your own case, you should think about what friends you have in the social spaces and what role they may play in growing your network and the time lag that there may be in getting the word out and converting them. By the time the Dockside Fundable site went live, the Dockside Facebook page had 1,195 likes, most of which would have been up to speed, more or less, on the intent of the project and the crowdfund.

Also shown in Figure 9 is the Railean Rum Facebook page. Railean makes some awesome rum from its artisan distillery in Railean, Texas, and is a friend of Eric's and sponsors his "Best of" CD. The rum is not yet distributed in Florida, but it might be someday. Railean could at some point become a Dockside partner, with Railean rum being served at Dockside and joint promotional events being set up on social media. The Railean Facebook page was not a huge part of driving traffic for the Dockside crowdfund, but it was left there as an illustration of another idea that might be useful in your crowdfund: to enlist close partner companies who may be buyers or suppliers in your business network.

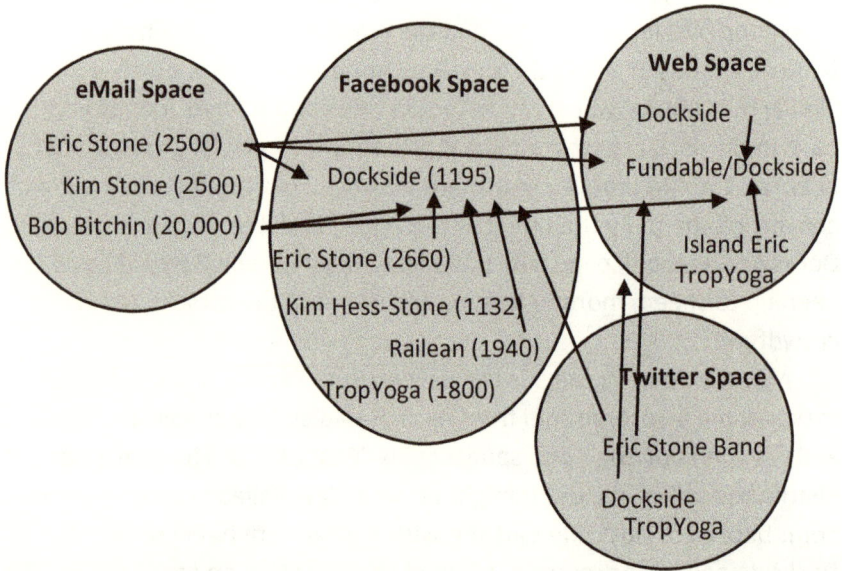

Figure 9: Interaction between Social Spaces

The Dockside Tropical Cafe Facebook page had approximately 1,195 likes at the time of the crowdfund. By the first day of 2014, it had 2,098 likes. The other numbers are estimates at the time of the crowdfund as well. The purpose of the diagram is to describe how different social spaces are related and to inform fans from across the spaces. In your application, other spaces or tools may fit in as well. The important things is that these other spaces be coordinated to bring traffic to the site where fans can participate in the fund itself. To simplify the illustration, Kim and Eric's use of LinkedIn was left out.

A final note about the network is that the social network you have developed for the purpose of crowdfunding now becomes a stronger network for supporting the next level of your endeavor. You will be able to use the network to communicate the development of your project and what projects will follow. In the case of Dockside, the obvious use of the network for the continued communication of what is going on at the restaurant is invaluable. Again, think of the crowdfund as a stepping stone in your bigger picture of developing community around your work.

Design and Implement the Social Platform

In Chapter 4, we described the what, why, and how for many of the popular social networking technologies. You need to make some choices about which are the best fit for your project. Consider which technology is used by your audience and which makes the best fit for what you want to communicate. Also, consider your time commitment to these technologies.

Once you have developed your own social networking plan, implement, test, monitor, and participate in the technologies well before crowdfunding so you will have some idea what your audience may be listening to and interested in during the crowdfund.

Integrate the Platform into Your Life

Keeping up with your virtual world can be difficult when you are running around in a complicated real world. Eric is always on the ready with his iPhone to shoot a pic and submit a post to Facebook. Make it easy and make it a habit and you can do a good job of keeping up.

Discuss Crowdfunding

Once you have a defined project and have an interested community, it is time to bring them into the discussion. Some in the community may not know much about crowdfunding while others may be familiar with crowdfunding but may not know how crowdfunding would move their project along.

As you set up your reward levels, share those ahead of time as well. Your audience may have suggestions for new levels and may suggest why some may or may not be designed as best as they could be. In some cases, you may have designed a reward well, but did not communicate it well, and your audience might misunderstand it. These are all good things to hear before you go live. Kim reminds me that some fans may have ideas that do not fit what you are trying to do and could become offended that their idea is not used.

Setup Crowdfunding

To setup the crowdfunding site, you need to first select a provider, design rewards levels, create a video and other crowdfunding site content, and presell the crowdfund. These steps need to be completed before your go-live date, so it will be important to choose a date and work backwards to figure out if it is reasonable to complete the work on time or if it will be necessary to adjust your timeframe.

Choose a Crowdfunding Provider

Eric and Kim chose Fundable and were happy with the results. They paid an extra consulting fee to Fundable, which may or may not have yielded return on investment (ROI). There is so much published today that you can read about. At the time of this writing, I was planning on crowdfunding with Kickstarter for little more than their big name. Kickstarter does have a "survey" tool that can be sent to backers at the end of the campaign in order to collect additional fulfillment information such as shirt sizes and mailing addresses. In Kim's fulfillment process, she had to rely on emailing fans for information that could not be collected directly from the Fundable site. Later, I changed the plan to use Indiegogo because Kickstarter does not allow books in the how-to business genre. Kickstarter's strategy is to remain more on the artistic side while Indiegogo has a more broad approach.

Since the field is changing rapidly, research the top sights and see if things are trending differently or if features have been added. Most of the sights are really quite simple in that they host your advertisement, let supporters select levels, and collect money. They are really less sophisticated than an eCommerce sites, like amazon.com or eBay, which is part of the reason they have begun to proliferate. For example, if you sell your product through Amazon.com, you can have amazon keep track of customers, payments, and fulfillment. At a crowdfunding site, much of the details of your rewards fulfillment will still be up to you. Once you have been through one crowdfund, or even read about one, you can see that a number of obvious features are missing. For example, there is little help with connections to social media or other types of marketing, and there is almost no help for fulfillment. As the sector grows, look for more sophisticated support to spring up. The need for more sophistication and new laws that make it easier to use, such as sites for equity investing, lead me to believe that 2014 and 2015 will bring about major changes in the additional support features offered by the crowdfund site. The message to you, the smart consumer of crowdfund services, is that you will have to recheck the research on this for your project.

Design Rewards Levels

Take a look at the range of rewards used by Eric and Kim. The goal here is to get price points that are appealing to different segments of your fan base. Try to imagine what the segments are like and put yourself in their shoes to see what might make an appealing reward level. Make a draft and talk to friends about it. If your list is substantially smaller than Eric and Kim's, start being creative and think about what would make a higher top-end level and what would make lower-entry level. If you have a substantial gap in price points, think of what could be added to the lower level. Ask yourself if partial products would be acceptable at lower price levels. Your top point can be pretty high. You don't have to be embarrassed if it goes unsold. The levels are a learning point for you because the response will teach you a lot about the real demand for your product.

Create a Video

Look at other videos first! There are plenty out there. Dissect the elements that make them work. They don't have to be in your field to lend great video tips. Eric showed me the crowdfund promotional video developed for Grapevine Craft Brewery, funded on Fundable in a campaign they started in May 2013[57]. Take a look at the video and see if you see some of the following points that Eric pointed out to me:

- Started with the history of beer, which gave more depth to the concept. Not all videos start with the history of beer, but it's a good way to break the ice. My technical editor joked that we should start with the history of the printing press. Watch our video to see if that idea makes the final cut. Eric, of course, was able to open with a nice history of Dockside Tropical Café, long a favorite watering hole of locals and tourists alike.
- Personal story with spouse. With Kim being Eric's wife as well as partner in the restaurant, the idea played well for them.
- Moving camera. Eric pointed out that the camera was always moving, giving a sort of a cinematic feel rather than home movie. Eric did some great camera work on his outside scenery shots.
- Commentary by prominent supporters.
- Outside shots of the community.
- The word community was used at least sixteen times in the Grapevine Beer video. I say at least. You try to count the word "community" while listening to the story of beer or watching the sandwich guy he interviewed. Actually, it could be a drinking game. Every time you hear the word community... well you know. Look for and use words that work for your mission.

Keep in mind that your audience knows a lot less about this project that you yourself have been immersed in for some time, so you will have to be clear about what you are doing. You have probably already explained this to friends over and over. It may be tempting to treat the video as an update to what many already know, but it needs to stand on its own. Focus on how your community becomes part of the project. Kim pointed out that the word "help" can make you sound needy, like you need someone else just to get this done, and maybe "assist" would be a better word.

The mechanics of creating a video have been substantially simplified by modern cameras, microphones, and software, but don't underestimate the time it will take if you are new to this. If you have a friend with more experience, this is a good time to call in a favor. What you will find is that, although modern video editing software is pretty easy to use, it is still more complicated than every day software, like word processors and spreadsheets. With video software, there are a million options buried under menus, and sometimes you will spend an hour finding the right one. The process of making the video involves writing the script, shooting and collecting the multimedia pieces, and assembling those pieces in video editing software. If you are new to this, you will find that you need to iterate through those three steps a couple or three times. Why? You will learn so much about the way you should have shot a scene after you try to edit it in the overall movie. Give yourself plenty of time and reach out to anyone in your circle that can assist you or take on the project themselves. If you are experienced with video editing, you may have a formula and sail through this.

Make sure you pre-sell the pre-sell. For many, the crowdfund will be dominated by the presale of items from your business. To allow you to come out of the shoot looking good, work with your closer fans to ask them to put in their orders on day one so that the crowdfund opens with some immediate sales. If you have some fans willing to do this ahead of time, make sure you give them a reminder on the day so that first day looks strong. This will give the more casual fans some confidence the effort will succeed. The amount of pre-sell pre-selling varies considerably, but consider 25% of what you need as reasonable.

Communicate Crowdfunding

Once the crowdfund goes live, regular communication is necessary to keep your fans apprised of the progress. In the beginning, make sure you announce on all the channels that you selected when you designed your platform. Make sure all of the channels have messages prepared, possibly some before you go live, because you will be busy keeping up with the communication.

One great way to communicate is to discuss the continuing development of the project. Most projects have had a certain amount of development prior to the crowdfund and will continue development during the crowdfund. Communicating where the project stands and what tasks or aspects of the project are being completed will help your community understand where the project is going and give them more confidence in you finishing the project. In Kim and Eric's case, they did a great job sending out pictures of Dockside. At the time of their crowdfund, the seller of the property had begun renovations that would be included in the sale. Pictures of those renovations and descriptions of why they were important to the project gave a dynamic buzz during the crowdfund period. You may be able to make the progress come alive with video. A friend of Eric's dropped by with a remote control helicopter that had a camera. He buzzed over the construction at Dockside and Eric posted the resulting video to Facebook. Even though the video quality was not superb, the great bird's eye view and the fun of a remote control helicopter made it a nice conversation piece. Kim suggests balancing humor and fun with the serious, matter of fact updates.

If other work or projects you do are closely related to the project being funded, you may want to keep people updated on those. For example, in the summer of 2013, Eric was on his summer tour and could update fans on how the tour was progressing. He also stopped in at the recording studio he works with in Nashville, another good event to share.

If you reach your goals early in the fund, you may want to consider stretch goals. Depending on your project, there may be more you can do if you reach even higher levels of funding. Be prepared to articulate the stretch goal once the initial goal has been met. Be clear on the amount of the next stretch goal and what will be done if you make it. Sometimes people will add a t-shirt for everybody if they make their stretch goal, but remember, reaching the stretch goal means you will have more orders to fulfill, and adding a t-shirt may make the margins too thin for you to follow through. It is also possible to have multiple stretch goals as each level has been met.

Develop Project

Usually the project is something that fits into the bigger picture of your dream. You now want to consider fulfilling the rewards in a timely way as well as leveraging the social platform for your future phases.

Pre-fulfillment Sub phase

Of course, before you can fulfill all those prepaid rewards, they need to be produced. Whether it is t-shirts, books, CD's, giftcards, or smart lightbulbs, you need to get the products produced. The key here is to plan before you launch the crowdfund. To what extent can you produce, or get ready to produce, before the crowdfund begins? Depending on the nature of your business, you may or may not be able to complete the design and prototype before the crowdfund. If you can finish the book or select the t-shirt, provide and produce a prototype before the crowdfund. Why? Because to the extent you can, you want to pull the trigger on manufacturing on the day the crowdfund ends. After completion of the crowdfund, you do not want to be in a position of selecting a t-shirt design, having a prototype printed, and possibly coming to the conclusion that the supplier needs to be changed, all while fans wait for rewards to be fulfilled. Since these things can be tested without the funding or knowing the quantity of funding, do it before the crowdfund time frame, and you can just update the quantity and pull the trigger on the order. In cases where you really need the funding to complete the prototype, make sure that was clear in your campaign and that the delays in fulfilling the rewards will result. In Kim and Eric's case, they needed to open a restaurant in order to fulfill the reward cards, and they needed the funds to complete the restaurant itself. They communicated this in the crowdfund. In terms of writing a book, you have to ask yourself if you really need the funds to write the book or just to print it? Does all of the book need to be funded, or is there one chapter that has a cost associated with it? Your fans will

121

appreciate the work that can be done ahead of time. Some writers get advances to write books, but it is often with a long track record and well developed proposal.

Chapter 6: One Month Later in Marathon

Well it is not a month later, and it is not Marathon, yet, but it seemed like a good title. I again headed out of New Orleans, but this time was different. The New Orleans airport bar was stocked with Bloody Mary mix, and, which I had not noticed before, olive infused vodka. This trip was getting started on the right foot. Touching down at the Key West airport, I found I could upgrade my economy car for a convertible Mustang for a small fee, which was hard to resist on a warm and sunny day in November. Well, I was traveling with a cute research assistant as well, increasing the need for a convertible. Also hard to resist was a night in Key West to prepare for interviews with Kim and Eric, the band, the staff, and the patrons. My assistant and I had an amazing meal at Manja Manja in Key West. They make their own pasta and sauces, and if you are stuck in Key West for a night on your way to Marathon, I highly recommend a dinner stop there.

We left Key West early the next morning, at about the crack of noonish, to head to Big Pine Key, a little less than thirty miles down the A1A in the direction of Marathon. We were at mile marker 0 in Key West, which is the only way to go on the A1A. Just off Duval is a little Cuban convenience store where we grabbed a sandwich and a coldie on the patio. It seems like it is hard to get out of Key West early or fast.

Anyway, we met up with the band at Rob's house in Big Pine Key where we found them already jamming up a storm. In addition to preparing the restaurant for opening, Eric had been putting together a new four piece band and was directing them in learning some of his over 160 original songs as well as helping them come together on covers they all knew. November 23, 2013, marks the first practice of the full four piece band, and it was, in fact, "Sunny and 85," as Eric's song about Dockside claims!

Rob was on guitar. Bob was on Bass, and John was on drums. Eric, of course, was on guitar and vocals. They were playing "Blackened Fish Sandwich." They started it about four times to get the right time. John kicked it in a little slow, and Eric said, "No, it has got to be faster." John kicked it up a notch and the band cruised through. Next they played, "Beer Money." The band seemed to be coming together well. Although the band had been studying Eric's music, this was the first time they were putting it all together, and it sounded amazing on its first run. "Beer Money" seemed stronger than with smaller arrangements, and seemed to benefit from the rock-kick the live drums and bass gave it. Next the band played some covers, including "Crossroads" and "No Woman, No Cry."

After practice was over, we headed to Dockside to check on repairs. Lijah was finishing up the cap on the foot rest on the water side of the bar, explaining the difficulty in getting the height right. The first one came out too low, and it certainly would not work to have a foot rest you could not reach from your barstool, so he remade it higher. Refitting the bar that had stood for many years and had been through many renovations was a very customized task.

After closing up the storm shutter, we headed over to Eric and Kim's place for some signature South of the Border burgers. We started with the famous fish dip and then Eric mixed up the burgers to his exact recipe and put them on the gas grill in the back. All the while, Kim was glued to her computer. Since 9 am, Kim had been configuring the point of sale (POS) system with every combination of drink order so they would be available to waitstaff for selection on their iPad POS device.

Think about it. Each drink, like a rum and coke or a mojito or whatever, multiplied by all the brands and levels of rum you could put in it, makes a lot of drink combinations. Once configured though, how cool that you can now do careful sale and inventory checking and the wait staff can just click on an order table-side and it will instantly show up at the bar, ready to be picked up when they get back. This is where the technology really makes living on island-time better. Just because you are at the beach doesn't mean your cold beverage should be delayed!

The next morning, we awoke early (9ish? 10ish? Who's counting?) for another day working in paradise. Kim was hitting it early, already making up the rewards cards to send out to the people that teamed up for crowdfunding. That work highlights a weakness of the current generation crowdfunding site. The sites have no connection to fulfillment. So when a fan goes to join a crowdfund, the site gathers their credit card information and the information needed to verify the credit card, name, and email address; next the project to be funded gets an Excel download with the funder's name, email address, and reward level. It is up to the funded organization, Dockside, in this case, or really Kim, who is in charge of crowdfund fulfillment, to email all of the fans for mailing addresses and other information, such as shirt size, before she can fulfill the orders. Since fulfillment may be months after the crowdfund, some people have changed mailing addresses and there is no easy way to get back in touch. The replies from the email come in slowly, so if a product has to be ordered in bulk, the people who responded quickly with fulfillment information still have to wait for the bulk of the email to come in. Note to crowdfunding providers: just let the funded organization define the fields of information needed for fulfillment and include those in the excel spreadsheet. The day the fund closes, some kind of fulfillment could be started.

At noon, some of the newly hired staff came by the house to help Kim pack t-shirts and hats! She reminded me to tell other crowdfunders to plan for the time needed to get rewards out. In Kim's case, that included 200 t-shirts, among other rewards. I would check in with her later that day to see how it went, but I was off to get a double Cuban coffee for motivation and then would head over to Dockside to check out activities there.

When I arrived at Dockside, Eric motioned me over and exclaimed, "Ken, check this out!" He showed me his iPad with an image of a mixing console, but it was not just an image. He touched the mixer slides, and he could control sound levels all over Dockside. People sitting at a table near the water, or close to the stage, or at the bar would all have appropriate sound level and accurate mixes from the premium Bose speakers and walk-around wireless level controls. We were rocking out to The Cars for the time being. Wait, can I say that. Don't show that line to Eric.

A little later, I was sitting at Dockside, at the edge of the dock next to the water, talking to John Otis, the drummer, for this incarnation of the Eric Stone Band. John had owned a sign company in Chicago and had become tired of making signs in Chicago, so he came down to the Keys. He had been living there off and on for years. When John and Eric were talking, Eric mentioned that he was auditioning for a drummer. John signed up for the audition and learned all the songs from the studio albums. To his surprise, he was the leading drummer after the audition. He thought there were two drummers in the competition.

John has been playing drums since he was around thirteen years old. His grandfather told him to play basketball, but John had no interest in that. He would go down in the basement and pound on the drums until his hands were blistered and bleeding. As I interviewed John, we gazed across Boot Key Harbor, and I couldn't get over the beauty of the place. Special blues and greens that aren't on the palette of the main land gently fluttered in the rippling wavelets. Rich green trees, mangroves, I had been told, stood on the mini islands that dotted the harbor. We could only see about twenty sailboats, but John told me that by high season, there would be hundreds. He said they would be anchored out in the ocean, waiting for slips or mooring balls in closer.

In his spare time, John liked to ferment pickles, preferring the kind without vinegar. You just use water and pickling salt, which has no iodine like table salt. Then you could add whatever you wanted to for flavor, like garlic, jalapenos, peppercorn, and dill seed. I asked John what his favorite ingredient was and he said he didn't have one. He made it different every time.

In the background, I could hear the scream of a circular saw cutting through the Tom Petty that was playing through the sound system. Around the back of the stage, Eric and some helpers were up to their ankles in sawdust, decimating some plywood into monitor cabinets. The monitor cabinets would house the stage monitors and would be covered in the same red carpet that was being used for the stage floor. The raised stage sat at the end of the main dining area with plenty of room in front for barefoot dancing. When you sat at a table, you could relish the view of the harbor and the sounds of the band equally, or you could dance on the dance floor with an old friend or new partner and let your imagination take you away in the moment.

Actually, watching all the hard work was making me thirsty. I grabbed a couple of coldies and motioned to Bob Jaeger, the bass player recruited for this version of the Eric Stone band, to come sit by a table near the water. He had made the move from New York, where he had experience with playing base as well as band promotion, and I was eager to get his perspective on the new band and the Key's music scene. I asked him how he was adjusting, and he gazed over Boot Key Harbor, with its playful ships and distant green mangroves and sighed, "Well, it doesn't get any better than this."

Bob had cut his teeth playing blues, swing, and funk. He picked up the bass guitar in high school when he found that there were more bands that needed bass than lead guitar and wanted to go where the opportunity was. He developed a love for the bass and enjoyed playing the bass line and holding down the bottom of the band. He later expanded his influence to promoting, primarily in the New York area. His promotion company got into providing the instruments and sound equipment for venues so that musicians could simply walk in and play, and he found this to be a good way to attract more and better musicians. One of the great things about Dockside is the sounds system and sounds stage that was designed by Eric himself and is a pleasure for musicians. Eric's years of playing venues that were not as well prepared for the band, resulting in poor quality listening environments for customers, made him determined to make Dockside both a musician's and a listener's quality environment.

In 2011, after plenty of visits to the Keys, Bob finally made the permanent move and started in Key Largo. Shortly after arriving, he went to an open-mike show, found a band, and started playing. Later, he met others and started a new band and moved to the Marathon area. When he saw Eric's Craig's list advertisement for a bass player, he was intrigued. He spoke with Eric and was impressed by the ground floor opportunity and wanted to help grow the new concept. In our interview, he said, "It has been exciting learning the new songs and learning Eric's precise lyrics. I can really relate to the lyrics from 'The Legend of the Lost Soul,' which strike a personal chord with me." Bob would soon grow his role into working the sound system at Dockside, managing Sunday open mike night, and helping to line up other bands.

Across the dock from us, Jeff, a future Dockside bartender and server, was putting together the new hightop table. Everybody was working on what they could to get the place open so they could get to their real jobs. The hightop tables had wood-looking tops and bamboo-looking legs, and they lined the wall behind the barstools on the inside. Paco, another future bartender, spread a syrupy varnish over the bamboo front of the bar, bringing a rich contrast between the dark and light hues in the bamboo.

Lijah, with experience in the brewing industry, had been hired to assist with operations management. He was showing me how the twelve tap systems works, saying it was kind of a pain with the twelve taps space so close together because some of the larger really cool tap handles banged into each other. In picking what beers to include, you have to consider meeting the range of tastes of the customers. He said, "Right now on tap, we have three lights, two reds, and are looking at how to fill in the others. We probably need an IPA. Probably a wheat needs to go in." He continued, saying, "We have the Sam Adams Cherry wheat coming in." In maintaining the system, he told me some of the sweet beers, like cider, screwed up the lines since they were harder to clean, but it could be handled. Yuengling would be on tap as well.

Back at the house, Kim was still packing up rewards, but by 7 pm, she took the rest of the night off. We celebrated the day with a few key lime pie martinis. What a concept. It is was smooth and creamy as the pie itself, but you could drink it. Kim told us we had just missed the key lime martini competition between the new bartenders to get the best recipe for Dockside. The final recipe ended up being a combination of the two best ones. The Dockside Punch competition followed.

The next morning, we loaded up the car with about fifty packages of rewards all addressed and labeled. The post office still scanned them individually and made a printed receipt so we would know what was shipped. After some amazing Cuban coffee that you can get at the Chevron station on Highway 1, we were ready to get back to work. The gas station was owned by Cubans who took great care in preparing the Café Con Leche and Espreso. It was amazingly strong, but not bitter. If you ask for sugar, you will get a lot.

One of the next hurdles to clear before opening to the public would be the health inspection. The health inspector confirmed that he would be back at 8 am the next morning. A bunch of the kitchen staff came back to make sure the kitchen would be ready to pass the health inspection.

Lija, the beer consultant, was now doing double duty installing lights that would shine up into the white tarp roof of the center eating area. The 30 watt LED would keep the ceiling lit without using much electricity. In general, Kim and Eric had been replacing conventional lights with LEDs as they remodeled in an effort to conserve energy and reduce monthly costs.

Already, there was a buzz around town that Dockside would be re-opening soon, and people were coming in more and more frequently to see the progress and offer assistance. People were already walking by and sitting down at tables. The staff had to tell them that it was not open yet. It would be easy to get some of this walk-in business. The board walk ran nicely through the center of Dockside, between the bar and the dock's eating area.

Back in the kitchen, the last minute cleanup was underway. The staff was getting organized and reviewing company policies to stay in compliance with health code. Every pan, utensil, and serving container was being washed. They were making good use of the dishwasher. There was some discussion as to which supplies belonged in which refrigerator.

A light rain was coming through. We could test how many of the tables would stay dry under the top during a rain. The lower wooden roof near the kitchen is a little more protected, so I could keep my laptop out during the rain. The rain and wind picked up a little. With all of the canvas open, a fine mist blew through. The tables along the water were a little wet.

Passed Health Inspection

We were all up early Tuesday, November 26 ,for the 8 am meeting with the health inspector. Dockside came through with flying colors and was now legally allowed to open. It was sunny, with a few puffy clouds, and 85 degrees. The view of Boot Key Harbor was outstanding. A fish jumped, a heron dived, and all was well at Dockside.

Eric connected some of the last network wires into the Breadcrum POS. Kim's late night data entry efforts with the full menu and drink list would be tested. This first day would be a little bit of a practice day, with just a few customers who had been around. The first rum drink was ordered.

Lijah was still working on lights. We definitely wanted some light for the first night of serving food. The servers were organizing the serving station. Erin was filling the pepper shakers. She was going to start with thirty-six shakers. At the moment, she didn't know where the salt was, so the salt shakers would have to wait. Mixed drinks were starting to flow, but the Coke was not coming out right. It would come out flat until the ice bins had cooled down for twenty minutes. They also had no change for cash orders. That would be fixed up soon. Checking the Coke tap a few minutes later, Eric remarked at how, with just a few degrees difference, it was working fine.

Jill was waiting on the first table. A relaxed couple took a table along the water. They ordered a Bacardi and diet and a Miller light with a cup of ice on the side. Their dog ordered an ice water in a bowl. She was served first while the humans waited on stuff in cups. They were paying with a credit card. This would be the first credit card. I was wondering if that would work. Eric put on a fresh tank top to be presentable and sat down for a minute with this first table couple. Smiles were ear to ear.

Being a small community, once the thumbs-up had been given to Kim and Eric, word spread. Since the Dockside boardwalk lead right into the restaurant, customers were already lining up, curious to see the competed venue after months of renovation. Dinghies were already pulling up as well. Most were just paddling across the still harbor, making for a serene, motorless approach

By 1 pm, a little chaos was starting to set in. The Sysco truck arrived and wheeled in the first food supplies. Bartenders were filling the ice bins and unpacking the bottled beer. One waiter quit and another was going on vacation, so Kim was juggling the schedule already. Waitresses were cleaning the plastic menu holders and inserting the newly printed menus that Kim had been editing only hours ago.

The first iteration of the menu would be somewhat limited to help the kitchen staff come up to speed. Including the fries, there were still eleven appetizers. I had already tried Smilin' Bob's Smoked Fish Dip, and it was outstanding. I thought the last vote was to serve it on a simple saltine which helped the dip flavor stand out. I was sure the buffalo conch and coconut shrimp would be awesome, too. Hog handles may have emerged as a specialty.

In two days, it would be Thanksgiving, so they would do a traditional cruisers Thanksgiving. Dockside would provide the turkeys and the waitstaff would volunteer. The cruisers would bring in their own sides and donate $5 to tip the wait staff.

Two couples dinghied up, looking like they were happy to have a little break from the boat. One man had the traditional white haired pony tail down his back (maybe not traditional on the mainland but easily fitting in there). All had dark sunglasses and flip flops. No high heels there. They stumbled off the front of their rubber dingy. The main dock of Dockside is just a little higher than the dinghies, so it was an easy step up. I'm not sure how much the sea level varies there. That is something to check.

Chapter 7: Sunset at Dockside

In late November 2013, Eric posted an ambitious Opening Week Event Calendar to mark the official grand opening of Dockside Tropical Café. Opening week celebrations even started at his concert at the Cruisers Outpost party at the St. Petersburg Power and Sailboat Boat show. At the party, we were all expecting the four piece Eric Stone Band, but it ended up being a six piece configuration with a local saxophone player and Shelly Hero, a former member of the early version of the band. All there were counting the days to the grand opening. It was day seven in the countdown to the much anticipated event.

St. Petersburg Power and Sailboat Show and Cruisers Party

On that December 7, sunny and 85 were the only thoughts in my head as I was walking the docks at the St. Petersburg Power and Sailboat Show when a cold front the size of the country, stretched from Dallas, TX, to Bangor, ME, rolled in. If I wasn't sure about how lucky I was to be there, a guy on the shuttle ride from the airport showed me a pic sent to his phone of Dallas covered in snow. Dodged that bullet! Of course, as I walked the docks at the boat show, I heard "Rock the Dock," which was playing at the floating bar, and the lyrics, "It's sunny and 85," wafting through the air. Darned if it wasn't sunny and 85. How did he do that?

Eric played the daytime show with his iPod tracks, affectionately know as, "Eric and the iPods." The harmonizer was actually labeled, "Shelly in a Box." Luckily that night, Shelly Hero would get out of the box, join the band in person, and we would enjoy her voice and high kicks!

I wandered the docks to try to figure out how many books I would need to sell to buy that new Beneteau. I love those big rectangular windows that they have been using for the past few years. I realized I didn't know how much it cost to produce a book, yet, so I couldn't figure it out. I posted the question to Facebook and a friend replied "more." Ok, well, that was enough math for one day.

To get some education, I went over to the seminar tents. The tattooed man was speaking. Larger than life and dressed in black, Bob Bitchin was regaling the audience with a "matter of fact" story about sailing with the king of somewhere. He met that guy while he was fixing his boat and found out they had a common interest in Harleys. Bob, at the time not knowing who the man was, stopped by the guy's boat, expecting to see his berth in the servants' quarters, and was treated to an evening of snacks and cocktails while being waited upon by the king's staff. In his seminar, Bob notes that the common bond between cruisers, particularly those with a circumnavigation under their belt, transcends socio-economic situations. I know I have really enjoyed the encouragement from new friends I have found in sailing, writing, and listening to Eric Stone that have made this journey really fun. However, you define your adventure, embrace your community, and enjoy the ride. Bob moved from riveting stories of his cruising adventures to sharing his and Jody's gratitude to the founding club members of their new magazine, *Cruising Outpost*, which was celebrating its first anniversary. In selling subscriptions to *Cruising Outpost*, money came in so fast at the beginning of the campaign that PayPal put a hold on the money to give them time to make sure it was not a scam. The move from his old magazine to the new one was once again an adventurous leap, but fans continued their support and made it work.

At 7 pm, the boat show closed down to give way to the cruisers' party, and Maria Elena Taylor asked me to dance. The free beer taps were opened, and I knew it would be a great evening. Bob and Jody have been hosting these cruiser parties for many years and at many boat shows around the country. Oh yeah. The new Eric Stone Band cranked it up in a six piece configuration for the night, which was my first time hearing the six piece version. The four piece new Eric Stone Band had been practicing for only a couple weeks. With great energy, they belted out a big chunk of Eric's massive library of original tunes. Shelly Hero, who had been playing with Eric as part of the Eric Stone Band Trio for many years, had joined them, along with Carl Dirkes on saxophone. The new Eric Stone Band was definitely bringing the house down, or rather, the tent; throw in Shelly on percussions and harmony, and a sax player, and you have magic. Shelly also brought the sex appeal of the band up a few notches as she tapped her tambourine on her butt and used a high kick to sound the cymbal.

Maria Elena came up with a team-plan for free pizza and beer and went to get pizza for the four of us. We were sitting with Gary and Shelly Howman. Gary would go for the beer. I would watch the chairs and Eric's CD sales table. I needed to hang around to do my book announcement. An excuse, yes, but I got the easy job on this play. Later, I would head up the beer run to redeem myself. I had only brought twenty-five copies of Chapter One to the show because I had only finished editing them that morning and had to go to the local Kinko's for printing. Printing costs were high.

Bob Bitchin did a great job of organizing the Cruisers Party and supporting all manufactures of the boat stuff on sale there. There was a great fundraiser raffle with sailor-oriented raffle items, from stainless steel cleaning products to trips to the Bahamas, and even a water maker, that would be great to have on the trip to the Bahamas. Dock 4, from St. Petersburg, seemed to rake in a ton of stuff. My new teammate in the beer pizza game, Gary Howman, won free hotel and dockage in the Bahamas for, I think, three nights. Despite Maria Elena's grand attempts at helping understand what tickets were in my range, I didn't come away with anything.

We danced the night away. We sang along to the Eric Stone lyrics like, "Blackened Fish Sandwich." We sang the anthem to Dockside, "Here's to you, here's to me." It seemed appropriate to jump in the air and raise your hands for each of those lines. Who knew Zepplin was trop rock? The end of the last set included some rocking out to some rock classics. Bitchin was yelling, "AC/DC!" Gary unleashed his ponytail and shook his long hair in hippy fashion. The other three of us followed, although we couldn't match his hair length.

Eric Stone Band closed with a powerful, "Rock the Dock," the song he wrote for Dockside.

After that, it was time to pack up. The Eric Stone Band, without Eric, had to get back to Dockside for the Sunday open mike the following afternoon. It would be their first performance without Eric. Eric stayed behind for a solo day at the boat show on Sunday.

It's Not Only Rock and Roll

On Sunday, the last day of the boat show, Eric played with his other band, "The iPods," until the 5 o'clock whistle blew. They really do blow a whistle to close out the boat show.

The last day of the boat show was kind of a winding down day. With a Goslings preferred beverage, I relaxed on the floating bar to a few sets of Eric's music. They actually ran out of the dark by the final day, and guests were relegated to the light. See, I told you it's not all fun and games.

Eric closed out with a searing solo, "Rock the Dock," and the last groups of fans cheered. I went to the stage and said happily, "It's only rock and roll!"

Eric replied, "No it's not. Look at all this stuff. It has to go on the Sprinter which is way over there." He pointed to some nebulous point that I would find out later was a hike down to the airfield where all the show's supply trucks were lined up.

136

Before we could head out with a load of stuff, Kim called with updates back at Dockside. Employee issues are an ongoing part of running a restaurant. Kim and Eric had hired some amazing staff, but this is a tough industry to hire and keep staff. I think everybody working in the bar and restaurant industry in the Keys has a story. With many of the staff coming from a wide variety of experiences and backgrounds, some who might be escaping something in the higher latitudes, sometimes causes problems of turnover or compatibility. For the staff that stay, sometimes it hard to decide who should be doing more or less leadership. Sometimes the staff with the skills or experience are the quieter ones who do not want to step on others toes. Then again, there are some that want to take charge a little too much. And as Eric told me, they all need to keep in mind that when they are in front of customers, "It's show time." This is a needed characteristic of staff if Dockside will fulfill its mission of having better customer service than the previous Dockside or many of the other island venues.

After conferring with Kim concerning Dockside, we made two trips, handfulls and cartfulls, out to the van. Eric hit the road by 7 pm, leaving the St. Petersburg show and starting the seven hour drive. He had a business to run the next morning at 8 am. I guess he's right. It's not always rock and roll.

The next day, I had to fly away from paradise, but I gave Kim a call from the Atlanta airport. She sounded like she was up to her neck in paperwork. She was not even sure how busy it was "out there," since she was confined to the office cubicle, but she was in great spirits anyway. The current hours of Docskside were 11-11, with the kitchen closing at 10 pm. Things were slower early and busier later. Business had ramped up amazingly fast.

After a brief departure to the mainland, I was able to return to Dockside for the remainder of opening week. When I arrived at Key West Airport, Garry Hass, Eric's west coast percussionist, and Kevin Wilkerson the PubClub blogger, graciously picked me up. The rum punches in the Key West airport are great. Tell them I sent you.

Garry and Kevin wanted to hit Key West the day before. Garry figured he needed to hit Key West while he was there and certainly catching sunset from Malory square was a much needed thing to do. I told him I liked watching the high rise sunset from the bar at the top of La Concha hotel. He told me it was better to watch a football game from field level, so he did the Malory Square thing. Lucky for me, he made it to the airport bar Friday morning and he, Gary, and I headed for Marathon. We did a little stop at the No Name Pub in Big Pine Key. That's a good stop. Don't tell Eric.

Each day throughout the Grand Opening week, there was music beginning in the afternoon, conch blowing contests, liquor tasting, and special guests.

The SV Jolly II Rover had sailed in from Key West. Designed by Naval Architect Merritt Walter, it was built in 1994 by Bock Marine of Beaufort, North Carolina[58,59]. This 80' square rigged schooner looked like a large pirate ship resting in front of the dingy area. Bill Malone bought her and refurbished her in 2003. After the refurbish, she lived in New Orleans, but Katrina blew her back to her current home in Key West. That day, it was just part of the fun having her at Dockside. BTW, the pic of her docked at Dockside received 151 likes in the first twenty hours after posting. Cool pictures work well on Facebook.

When we arrived at Dockside, Eric said, "This place is going crazy."

Lijah said, "It's a mess," referring to the chaotic scene. Dockside was hopping, and it was a little crazy, but it was great to see the crowd having a good time.

While waiting for 7 pm and Eric Stone Band, we put away some hog handles. They were good. A little like a rib. Tender slow cooked pork, best if eaten with some Dockside hot sauce on it.

After the first band, Island Time, played, a hard rain came down. A couple drops passed by the tarp, but no problem, mon. Next year, Eric hoped to do the full tiki roof, but they were expensive.

At 7 pm, the band started to warm up. Yep. It was Eric Stone Band, opening with,"Rock the Dock!" He also managed a happy birthday for a patron.

When he played, "The Legend of the Lost Soul," some of the belly rubbing started. Eric also joked that he played both kinds of music, "country and western." He played the famous David Allen Coe anthem, "Meet Me in Mooloolaba." Next he rocked out to a little Petty. Although the band was well versed in Eric's extensive original catalog, they were versatile at other covers as well.

Gary was in it and could really conga up Eric's song, The Lunar bar. That was groovy. Although the night was young, at 8 pm, many were still chowing away at some awesome food, which weighs you down. But many couples came and danced their version of everything from surfing dances to almost fifties-like jitterbugging. What's that thing guys do with an air guitar? Then Clapton's, "You Look Wonderful Tonight," did draw a bunch of couples to the floor. I screamed Zeppelin between sets and the band laughed. They had rocked out to it in St. Petersburg. Wait. Now he was kicking in, "Brown Eyed Girl." The pirates really dug that. Sometimes it transitioned into some harder rock. And that was the first set. I couldn't wait for the second.

The band ended, and they debriefed on how they could get better. Eric wanted to delegate song timing to the drummer. If he could get an easy way to use a visual metronome, he could punch in the correct song timing and John could lead in it. When they pick the best speed for "Blackened Fish Sandwich," John would punch it in, and the band would fire at that speed.

Grand Opening Closes to a New Beginning

Sitting on the edge of the dock on that final evening of opening week, I stared out at the little yellow sailboat that had been moored in the harbor, seemingly observing the festivities all week. The sailboat swayed back and forth with the changes in the wind, sometimes presenting her starboard side and sometimes her port, and in between, she was looking straight at us. She seemed to be straining to come over for a visit. Luckily, we, being people, can untie are own mooring lines, sail the seas, and stop at new ports. I hope her owner is taking good care of her.

The sun set on Boot Key Harbor with a warm orange glow in the sky. The serenity seemed to be the reward for a week well done by Kim, Eric, and the staff. It may have been chaos, but for the most part, it worked, and many friends were made. Dockside was certainly off to an auspicious beginning. Where she actually sails is to be seen and whether Kim and Eric call for a tack is not yet known, but they have most certainly cut the dock lines.

Eric and Kim's adventure was launched through the power of crowdfunding. A little bit of support and love from a whole lot of people equals a whole lot of love and support. The old saying, "It takes a village to raise a child," can certainly be applied to crowdfunding. Each individual that uses crowdfunding as a way to "raise their child" has the advantage of a support system that puts them ahead of the game. The key thing to remember is that the crowdfunding websites and software are just tools. You, the entrepreneur, must enable an effective social process.

End Notes

[1] Partial lyrics from "Rock the Dock" (Stone, Rock the Dock., 2013)
[2] (Schawbel, 2012)
[3] (Massolution, 2013)
[4] (Crowdfunding.org, 2013)
[5] Location 57, (Aversa, 2013)
[6] (Fundable, 2013)
[7] (Kickstarter, 2013)
[8] (EquityNet, 2013)
[9] Sullivan listed Alexas data for the ten sites where data is listed. Comparable data was not found for the other sites. See (Sullivan, 2013).
[10] (Knowledge@Wharton, 2010)
[11] (Knowledge@Wharton, 2010)
[12] (Knowledge@Wharton, 2010)
[13] (Ghose, 2012)
[14] (Wikipedia, n.d.)
[15] (Ghose, 2012)
[16] (Fundable, 2013)
[17] (Ha, 2014)
[18] (Baio, 2009)
[19] (Baio, 2009)
[20] (Schawbel, 2012)
[21] (Kolodny, 2014)

---

[22] (Heins)

[23] (Heins)

[24] (Stone, 2013)

[25] In 2014, the Strictly Sail Chicago Boat Show merged with the Chicago Boat, RV and Outdoors show to form the Chicago Boat, RV, and Strictly Sail Show.

[26] (Hess-Stone, n.d.)

[27] (Hess K. N., 2007)

[28] (Hess, Why Kim Hess Got Her Captain's License, 2009)

[29] (Hess, 2010)

[30] http://www.well.com/

[31] (Raggett, 1998)

[32] http://www.w3.org/People/Raggett/book4/ch02.html

[33] http://www.w3.org/

[34] (Google, 2009)

[35] Sithsonian.com, (accessed 8/25/2013), http://www.smithsonianmag.com/science-nature/The-Top-Ten-Weirdest-Dinosaur-Extinction-Ideas-218400531.html

[36] Blogger, About page, accessed 8/30/2013. https://www.blogger.com/about.

[37] (Bilton, 2013)

[38] (Drupal, n.d.)

[39] (Wikipedia, 2013)

[40] (Henry, 2013)

[41] Forked is a computer term for taking the development of a piece of software in a new direction.

[42] Wikipedia, Matt Mullenweg, accessed 8/31/2013. http://en.wikipedia.org/wiki/Matt_Mullenweg.

[43] (Gannes, 2012)

[44] (PingDom, 2012)

[45] See (de Valk, 2013)

[46] (de Valk, 2013)

[47] (Grahl, 2013)

[48] Holmes, R. FastCompany, http://www.fastcompany.com/3002170/email-new-pony-express-and-its-time-put-it-down

[49] (Wikipedia, 2013)

[50] (Instagram, n.d.)

[51] (Systron, 2013)

[52] (Crook, 2013)

---

[53]   Wikipedia, Aspect Ratio (Image), accessed 8/3/2013. http://en.wikipedia.org/wiki/Aspect_ratio_%28image%29.

[54] (Alexa, 2013)

[55] (Wilkinson, n.d.)

[56] http://www.dolphins.org/

[57] http://www.fundable.com/grapevine-craft-brewery

[58] Learn more about the Jolly Rover at: http://schoonerjollyrover.com/

[59]   Learn more about Merrit Walter and his schooners at: http://www.roverschooners.com/

References

Alexa. (2013, September 13). *About*. Retrieved from Alexa:
    http://www.alexa.com/company
Aversa, A. (2013). *The Ultimate Kickstarter Guidebook: A Proven
    Formula for Crowdfunding Success* (First Edition ed.).
Bilton, N. (2013). *Hatching Twitter: A True Story of Money, Power,
    Friendship, and Betrayal*. New York: Portfolio/ Pneguin.
Blood, R. (2000, September 7). *Weblogs: a History and Perspective*.
    Retrieved September 2, 2013, from Rebeccrebeccablood.net:
    Blood, Rebecca. 2000. "Weblogs: a History and
    Perspective,http://www.rebeccablood.net/essays/weblog_histo
    ry.html
Crook, J. (2013, September 8). *Topping 140 M users, Instagram promises
    ads within the next year*. Retrieved September 9, 2013, from
    TechCrunch.
Crowdfunding.org. (2013, September 13). *Crowdfunding Directory*.
    Retrieved from Crowdfunding.org:
    http://www.crowdsourcing.org/directory
de Valk, J. (2013, August 30). *WordPress SEO: The Definitive Guide To
    Higher Rankings For WordPress Sites*. Retrieved September 29,
    2013, from http://yoast.com/:
    http://yoast.com/articles/wordpress-seo/

Drupal. (n.d.). *About Drupal*. Retrieved 9 24, 2013, from Drupal:
    https://drupal.org/about

Empson, R. (2012, April 5). *With JOBS Act Becoming Law, Crowdfunding
    Platforms Look To Create Self-Regulatory Body*. Retrieved
    September 13, 2013, from TechCrunch:
    http://techcrunch.com/2012/04/05/with-jobs-act-becoming-
    law-crowdfunding-platforms-look-to-create-self-regulatory-
    body/

EquityNet. (2013, 9 13). *Company Overview*. Retrieved from EquityNet:
    https://www.equitynet.com/aboutus.aspx?lnk=1

Fundable. (2013, September 13). *Preparing for Equity Fund Raising*.
    Retrieved from Fundable:
    http://www.fundable.com/faq/preparing-for-equity-fundraising

Fundable. (2013, September 13). *Rewards or Equity*. Retrieved from
    Fundable: http://www.fundable.com/faq/rewards-or-equity

Gannes, L. (2012, April 25). *Automattic Grows Up: The Company Behind
    WordPress.com Shares Revenue Numbers and Hires Execs*.
    Retrieved September 1, 2013, from All Things D:
    http://allthingsd.com/20120425/automattic-grows-up-the-
    company-behind-wordpress-com-shares-revenue-numbers-and-
    hires

Ghose, C. (2012, July 20). *One of five first Fundable campaigns meets
    crowdfunding goal; later startups surged*. Retrieved from
    Columbus Business First:
    http://www.bizjournals.com/columbus/news/2012/07/20/one-
    of-five-first-fundable-campaigns.html?page=all

Google. (2009, September 21). *Google does not use the keywords meta
    tag in web ranking*. Retrieved September 29, 2013, from Google
    Web Master Central Blog:
    http://googlewebmastercentral.blogspot.com/2009/09/google-
    does-not-use-keywords-meta-tag.html

Grahl, T. (2013). *You First 100 Copies: The Step-by-Step Guide to
    Marketing Your Book*. Tim Grahl.

Ha, A. (2014, March 13). Fundable Acquires LaunchRock To Combine Crowdfunding And User Acquisition. Retrieved June 18, 2014, from TechCrunch.com: http://techcrunch.com/2014/03/13/fundable-acquires-launchrock/

Heins, J. (n.d.). *Eric Stone Biography.* Retrieved September 9, 2013, from All At Sea Magazine: http://www.islanderic.com/bio.html

Henry, A. (2013, February 18). *Posthaven Offers Posterous Refugees a Replacement that Will Never Shut Down (Because You're Paying for It).* Retrieved September 18, 2013, from lifehacker: http://lifehacker.com/undefined

Hess, K. (2009, August 29). *Why Kim Hess Got Her Captain's License.* Retrieved 12 29, 2013, from Women and Cruising: http://www.womenandcruising.com/blog/2009/08/why-kim-hess-got-captains-license/

Hess, K. (2010, June 4). *Kim Hess Moves Aboard Her First Boat.* Retrieved 12 29, 2013, from Women and Cruising: http://www.womenandcruising.com/blog/2010/06/kim-hess-moves-aboard-her-first-boat/

Hess, K. N. (2007). *Yoga Aboard.* Blue Duck Enterprises.

Hess-Stone, K. (n.d.). *About Kim.* Retrieved 12 29, 2012, from Tropic yoga: http://www.tropicyogaandsailadventures.com/about-kim/

Instagram. (n.d.). *About Us.* Retrieved October 1, 2013, from Instagram.

Kelly, M. (2013, August 29). *Kickstarter campaigns raise 6x more than Indiegogo, says researcher.* Retrieved from VentureBeat: http://venturebeat.com/2013/08/29/kickstarter-campaigns-raise-6x-more-than-indiegogo-says-researcher/

Kickstarter. (2013, September 13). *What is Kickstarter?* Retrieved from Kickstarter: http://www.kickstarter.com/hello?ref=nav

Knowledge@Wharton. (2010, December 8). *Can You Spare a Quarter? Crowdfunding Sites Turn Fans into Patrons of the Arts.* Retrieved from Knowledge@Wharton:

http://knowledge.wharton.upenn.edu/article.cfm?articleid=264
7

Lee, S. (2013, September 11). *The Newest Hottest Spike Lee Joint*. Retrieved from Kickstarter: http://www.kickstarter.com/projects/spikelee/the-newest-hottest-spike-lee-joint

Lunden, I. (2012, June). *Analyst: Twitter Passed 500M Users In June 2012, 140M Of Them In US; Jakarta 'Biggest Tweeting' City*. Retrieved July 30, 2013, from TechCrunch.

Massolution. (2013). *The Crowd Funding Industry Report*. Retrieved September 10, 2013, from http://www.crowdsourcing.org/editorial/2013cf-the-crowdfunding-industry-report/25107

PingDom. (2012). *PingDom*. Retrieved August 31, 2013, from WordPress completely dominates top 100 blogs: http://royal.pingdom.com/2012/04/11/wordpress-completely-dominates-top-100-blogs/.

Raggett, D. L. (1998). *Raggett on HTML 4*. Addison Wesley Longman.

Schawbel, Dan. (2012). "Indiegogo's Cofounder On The Wisdom Of Crowdfunding," *Forbes,* October 22.

SquareSpace. (2013). Squarespace.com, About page. Retrieved September 10, 2013 from http://www.squarespace.com/about/company.

Stone, E. (2013). *Episode 1: Time to Fly*. Retrieved September 06, 2013, from Eric Stone Radio: http://www.ericstoneradio.com/

Stone, E. (2013, April 25). *Episode 4, Interview with Kenny Royster*. Retrieved September 9, 2013, from Eric Stone Radio: http://www.ericstoneradio.com/.

Stone, E. (2013, April 7). *Eric Stone Radio*. Retrieved September 8, 2013, from Episode 2, Nashville & 24 Meets 40," Eric Stone Radio (podcast): http://www.ericstoneradio.com/.

Stone, E. (2013). *Rock the Dock*.

Sullivan, M. (2013, September 13). *Crowdfunding*. Retrieved from PBWorks:

http://crowdfunding.pbworks.com/w/page/10402176/Crowdfu
nding

Switek, B. (2013, August 6). *The Top Ten Weirdest Dinosaur Extinction Ideas.* Retrieved August 25, 2013, from Smithsonian.com:
http://www.smithsonianmag.com/science-nature/The-Top-Ten-Weirdest-Dinosaur-Extinction-Ideas-218400531.html

Systron, K. (2013, June). *Video.* Retrieved October 1, 2013, from Instagram Blog:
http://blog.instagram.com/post/53448889009/video-on-instagram

Wikipedia. (2013, October 4). *MailChimp.* Retrieved from Wikipedia: http://en.wikipedia.org/wiki/MailChimp

Wikipedia. (2013, 09 23). *Movable Type.* Retrieved from Wikipedia: http://en.wikipedia.org/wiki/Movable_Type

Wikipedia. (n.d.). *Compact Disk.* Retrieved September 8, 2013, from Wikipedia: http://en.wikipedia.org/wiki/Compact_disc.

Wikipedia. (n.d.). *Fundable.* Retrieved September 13, 2013, from Wikipedia: http://en.wikipedia.org/wiki/Fundable

Index

www.ingramcontent.com/pod-product-compliance
Lightning Source LLC
Chambersburg PA
CBHW031404180326
41458CB00043B/6608/J